KEEPING FAITH
WITH HOPE

Where are sustainable possibilities of peace with justice to be found in Israel–Palestine, tragically divided as it is between two peoples and three faiths? In the face of continuous, entrenched cycles of conflict can one maintain both a sense of perspective and a stance of realistic hopefulness? This book addresses the key issues embraced by those profound questions in thoughtful, practical ways.

Gathering together dispatches and commentary over a period of nearly twenty years from international lawyer, independent diplomat and engaged ecumenist Dr Harry Hagopian, *Keeping Faith With Hope* blends experience and insight in often-unexpected ways.

By interweaving the political, the personal and the spiritual, the author opens up new paths for understanding what is going on in Israel–Palestine and how we might engage more fruitfully with the region in the future. Here is both a testament to hope and a living exemplification of it.

Harry Hagopian is an international lawyer, ecumenist and political consultant. He also acts as Legal Consultant to OTS Solicitors in London (particularly on Brexit and immigration issues). He is an Ekklesia associate and regular contributor. Formerly Executive Secretary of the Jerusalem Inter-Church Committee and Executive Director of the Middle East Council of Churches, Dr Hagopian has been Middle East, North Africa and Gulf adviser to the Catholic Bishops' Conference of England and Wales. He is author of *The Armenian Church in the Holy Land* (The Russell Press).

To the two peoples and three faiths of the Holy Land. May hope never die out

KEEPING FAITH WITH HOPE

THE CHALLENGE OF ISRAEL–PALESTINE

HARRY HAGOPIAN

Ekklesia

First published in June 2019

Ekklesia
235 Shaftesbury Avenue
London
WC2H 8EP
www.ekklesia.co.uk

Production and design: Bob Carling (www.carling.org.uk)
Managing Editor: Simon Barrow

ISBN: 978-0-9932942-7-3

The cover: *The Via Dolorosa* (Latin for 'Way of Grief', 'Way of Sorrow', 'Way of Suffering' or simply 'Painful Way') is a processional route in the Old City of Jerusalem, believed to be the path that Jesus trod on the way to his crucifixion.

Contents

Acknowledgements

Many are the men and women who have impacted my Israeli-Palestinian journey over the years.

However, for the purposes of this book, I would like to thank Simon Barrow, who both as friend and editor, has done a remarkable job of pulling the various components of this book together. He has put up with my comments with composure, understanding and bonhomie!

Also a big word of thanks to Rami G. Khouri: forget his embarrassingly wonderful Foreword to my book – Rami and I have known each other for decades, and our first public discussion on Israel–Palestine was when he interviewed me on his Encounter programme on Jordan TV2 (English) many moons ago. Rami's thinking impacts not only Israel–Palestine but the whole MENA-Gulf region, and he is a beacon of hope for many Arab men and women.

I cannot forget HB Michel Sabbah, Patriarch Emeritus of the Latin-rite Catholic Church in Jerusalem. Nor can I stress enough the plethora of conversations he and I had in his office in Jerusalem when I was representing the 13 traditional churches in the ecumenical and political negotiations. Politically vulnerable as I was at times, he always had my back and was a wonderful teacher who was so confident in both his Palestinian and Christian identities.

I also owe a lot to Gabi Habib, a former general secretary of the Middle East Council of Churches. I was his assistant, but he was my ecumenical tutor who introduced me to a range of Christian traditions, with their strengths and weaknesses. But he was also my coffee mate: there was nothing more uplifting than having an Arabic cup of coffee with him (that I always prepared myself!) almost every morning in order to discuss the items on our common agenda.

I could go on and on, but I will stop here by keeping the biggest generic 'thank you' to the ordinary Palestinians – Muslims and Christians alike – who never tired from explaining to me the intricate challenges of Israel–Palestine. They are the unknown soldiers of this unjust and enduring conflict.

Publisher's Preface

Where are sustainable possibilities of peace with justice to be found in Israel–Palestine, tragically divided as it is between two peoples and three faiths? In the face of continuous, entrenched cycles of conflict, can one maintain both a sense of perspective and a stance of realistic hopefulness? This book addresses the key issues embraced by those profound questions in thoughtful, practical ways.

Gathering together dispatches and commentary over a period of nearly twenty years from international lawyer, independent diplomat and engaged ecumenist Dr Harry Hagopian, *Keeping Faith With Hope* blends experience and insight in often-unexpected ways.

By interweaving the political, the personal and the spiritual, the author opens up new paths for understanding what is going on in Israel–Palestine and how we might engage more fruitfully with the region in the future. Here is both a testament to hope and a living exemplification of it – one that Ekklesia is both proud and honoured to publish.

Dispatches from the front

What you now have in your hands is a unique document. The author manages to combine that sense of immediacy and colour which comes from the best on-the-ground engagement with a high level of background knowledge and expertise. As well as detailed information and thoughtful analysis, his 'dispatches from the front' also offer important elements of personal experience, storytelling, a human touch and good humour.

It has not been easy distilling, selecting and combining almost one hundred articles over a twenty-year period for this volume. What I have tried to capture most of all is the important sense of journey this book and its author embodies. The material has been gathered and edited principally from Dr Hagopian's own website, *Epektasis* (www. epektasis.net) – a Greek word which has been rendered "striving" in the New Testament (Philippians 3.13), but which also reflects the doctrine of unceasing evolution in that happiness which comes from God alone, as developed by St Gregory of Nyssa.

This combined sense of purposeful struggle and receiving the (often surprising) solace of the divine is highly appropriate. It captures well the author's own travails – personal, political and spiritual – and it also mirrors the multiple examples of hope and striving which make up the complex, painful and human story of Israel Palestine itself.

A continuing conversation

Alongside pieces penned for Dr Hagopian's own substantial network of contacts across the globe are those written or adapted for an even wider audience. These include thoughts and reflections offered to the *Huffington Post*, to Ekklesia, to the BBC, to Al Jazeera and to numerous other global outlets for news and commentary.

What holds the collection together (apart from the thematic organisation) is the author's determination to face reality and to name tragedy, while at the same time recognising in the flux of events the continual possibilities of change, transition and transformation. Ultimately it is people who make both faith and hope doable, and it is therefore people who lie at the heart of the portrait Dr Hagopian offers and the analysis he brings.

It is our hope in publishing this book that the wisdom and insight it brings will be a stimulus to ongoing conversation and engagement both among those with deep knowledge and experience in the region and among those looking in from the outside who wish to have their understanding enriched and their assumptions challenged.

Simon Barrow
Director, Ekklesia

Foreword

Amid the shrill shouting matches and escalating inability of most players in the Israel–Palestine conflict to acknowledge the legitimate needs of the other, one sometimes despairs to hear a voice of reason that suggests a path out of the stalemate and mutual recriminations. The decades that I have known Dr Harry Hagopian and followed his work and writings make him for me a leading candidate for that 'voice of reason' designation, which is why I am so pleased to see this collection of his thoughts in a single anthology.

Harry is very rare when it comes to analysts, observers, or engaged practitioners in the Israel–Palestine conflict, due to the array of experiences and expertise that he embodies. I say this with confidence because I have known or followed the work of virtually all the major actors in this conflict in my half a century of personal, political, and journalistic engagement in Arab-Israeli issues – starting from my university days in the late 1960s.

Harry is worth listening to when he speaks or writes on this issue because his rare combination of attributes touch on all the critical arenas that define this conflict. His worldview and work are deeply anchored in his first hand knowledge on the ground of both the human and territorial dimensions of the conflict. His many years of living in Jerusalem have etched into his mind and heart the legitimate needs, rights, and demands of both Israelis and Palestinians. His personal contacts among Palestinians, Israelis, other Arabs, and international actors capture the wider context that will be needed to forge a just and permanent peace one day.

This multi-dimensional, lived-life perspective is bolstered by the three value scales that have defined his entire adult life: his legal training and work across countries; his faith-based ecumenical endeavours in the Middle East and abroad; and, his relentless quest for possible political breakthroughs in track two diplomacy, workshops, and other gatherings where Palestinians, Israelis, and supportive outsiders have sought diligently – but futilely, to date – to resolve the conflict in a manner that simultaneously honours the dictates of faith, law, history, geography, and a shared humanity.

All these dimensions one day must shape a permanent peace agreement. Until then, Harry Hagopian's analyses and suggestions – always calm, factual, equitable – are a welcomed voice of reason that points out honestly our errant political actions, and reminds us of the critical core realities for both sides that can and must be reconciled. His enduring message is that a century-long conflict by the hands of men and women can be ended by those same people's hands, hearts, faith, and commitment to the rule of law, harnessed and inspired by quality leaderships.

Rami G. Khouri
American University of Beirut
www.ramikhouri.com

Introduction: Travelling in Hope

This is an account of the ongoing struggle to help find a path towards peace in Israel–Palestine. It is therefore a book about journeying – sometimes linear, often uneven and apparently meandering, but woven together by the contours of faith, the persistence of hope and a sense of justice. So in offering these reflections on the region, I need to say something about how this story is not external to me but part of my own journeying over many years.

Beginning with diversity

I was born in Jerusalem, which at that time, in the early 1960s, was part of Jordan. My parents were both Armenian, and I was raised not only to learn the language but also to observe the traditions of both the Armenian Orthodox and Armenian Catholic churches. I also came into the world at a time when there was peace. My memories of Jordan as a toddler were those of happy quietness. We did not live in the Armenian Quarter of the Old City but in the northern hilly suburbs of Jerusalem alongside many other Muslim and Christian neighbours. I remember running around the garden, climbing up the almond or plum trees or riding my bicycle with friends and everything felt normal for a kid whose family made sure he was fine.

By being born when and where I was, I was reproducing two things in my life. First, I discovered that I was and am a product of what happened to my forefathers during the Armenian genocide of 1915, and about which I have written extensively. My grandparents and my great grandparents were living in Ottoman Turkey at the time of those massacres and they fled to settle in Lebanon, then in mandated Palestine and finally in Jordan. That is how I got to be who I am. Second, I was and am marked by my 'Armenian-ness', if I can put it that way – the language, the culture, the faith, the churches I used to attend with my parents. Sometimes we would go to the Catholic Church and sometimes to the Orthodox. However, my family did not raise me as a young boy living in an Armenian bubble. In fact, quite the opposite, as we lived in an Arab Palestinian neighbourhood, where a lot of our friends were not Armenian, and so I do not think I could describe myself – even at that tender age – as being ethnocentric.

This moving between worlds, countries and traditions seemed natural to me because of the way I was brought up and the experiences I had over many decades. My ecumenical journeying later in life has its bearings here, and also my approach to what is happening across the Middle East and North Africa (MENA) region up to this day. The way forward has to involve crossing boundaries, because this is how we learn who we are, who the other is, and how we might live together. Now some people might ask "how did you sort all this out?" But I would regard that as the wrong question. If anything, I would want to say that through the intersecting paths that created me, coupled with my own upbringing, the Holy Spirit was giving me the strength to carry on. I didn't need to do all this on my own. I needed only to realise, at a deeper level, who I was and where and why I was being led.

Moving forward, when I was a young teenager I was fortunate that my parents were willing to let me leave the region alone and travel to France to continue my education. This is a country with the largest Armenian community in Europe, so I went and stayed with an Armenian-French family. That is where I grew up, where I was educated and where I did my pre-university studies. It is where I learnt about 'the French way' of being and fell in love for the first time as a spotty kid with a fellow French student! But then out of what could be called a whim, I decided, when talking to some friends, that I would enter university in the UK. There was ostensibly no objective reason for that choice, but once again it offered me a whole new series of life lessons. So I completed a law degree in Manchester, and then went on to complete a Doctorate in Public International Law and a Masters in Conflict Resolution. This was ideal for me, because I was fascinated by how states operated, how treaties were formed and reformed, and what human rights meant.

Ecumenical explorations

I then spent some time in legal practice, being head-hunted into work on patents and trademarks. That involved commuting between Beirut in Lebanon and Nicosia in Cyprus, being responsible for the company's interest in intellectual property rights across the Middle East, North Africa and Gulf regions. That gave me yet another set of footholds in, and perspectives on, the region. When I started these travels, for instance, I recall that the airport in Dubai was basically a metallic shack compared with its impressive structure today. Things in the 1980s in Yemen and Iraq were also very different to the turmoil that followed in the 1990s. Lebanon had emerged from a nasty civil war, and the Palestinian problem was slowly 'internationalising' its appeal. So when people tell me that they discovered the MENA region via the so-called

Arab Spring, I smile and am tempted to tell them that I got to know this region way before those forces of freedom went out into the streets and also before they were quashed by counter-revolutionary forces.

This 'keeping moving' is in some respects part of the Armenian DNA – not to settle down in a way that you become sedentary in any one place. So I decided to make another shift, in spite of having what commercially would seem like a very successful and lucrative career. Again I was head hunted, this time by the Middle East Council of Churches (MECC). I was assistant general secretary to Gabriel Habib for almost five years in the late 1980s. Gabi, a Lebanese Byzantine Christian, was a great teacher as well as communicator, and this was a *kairos* moment for me, a radical turning point in my life, exposing me to yet more situations and experiences through the lens of a faith which is at one and the same time deeply rooted and migratory, singular and diverse. It brought fresh challenges that were also fresh opportunities. What I was caught up in here was no longer the trajectory of growing up, but a set of worlds that required a new language. This is where I first heard the word 'ecumenical', or *oikumene* – with its dual emphasis on "the whole inhabited earth" as God's concern, and also the search of the churches for a common life and witness in respect of that. I had, of course, been brought up in an ecumenical albeit Armenian way, but I had not labelled it that way, nor had I thought through the implications of living that open way consciously and deliberately, while retaining one's identity and sense of belonging with a people.

This is when I suddenly began to discover the huge breadth and richness of Christian tradition and history – whether it is the Eastern Orthodox, the Oriental Orthodox, the Western Catholics, the Eastern Catholics, the Anglicans, Lutherans, and various other Protestants as well as more. What I came to appreciate is that all these people were what made up the Middle East Council of Churches, and my role as assistant to the MECC general secretary was to be involved with all of them. In return, these churches introduced me to a whole new dimension of my own faith, which until that point had been a very private and personal thing. Now it began to recognise and embrace a strong public aspect. In helping the MECC to function I found myself involved with programmatic work on refugees, human rights, unity among the churches and the vital outreach with other churches and church organisations outside the Middle East, North Africa and Gulf regions. At the same time, the aim of the MECC was – and remains to be – an instrument of the churches and a point of cooperation, not a church in and of itself. Therefore, it does what its members want it to do, which is to facilitate their work 'at the crossroads', so to speak. That involved for example major humanitarian and ecclesial challenges in Lebanon and Iraq after the two Gulf wars as well as in Iran following an earthquake.

Serving the process

After serving at the MECC I returned to the UK to undertake some more legal work. But I soon discovered that shuffling paperwork was not really what I wanted to do, and I was fortunate enough to find another opportunity. This time it was the Heads of the Churches in Jerusalem who approached me. They knew me from my family connections, but also from my work at the Middle East Council of Churches. What they wanted was assistance with the second track negotiations as part of the Oslo Chapter of the peace process from the mid- to early 2000s. I became executive director of the MECC office in Jerusalem, handling programmatic work as well as responsible pilgrimages to the Holy Land from the USA and Europe. I also was playing the political role of helping to protect the interests of the 13 traditional churches in the Holy Land. At the same time, I set up a body called the Jerusalem Inter-Church Committee (JICC) which was independent of ecumenical bodies and concerned itself directly with the churches themselves. JICC enabled me to interact with the Oslo process on the basis of guidance and support from my board. I continued to work in this way until the early 2000s when, sadly, the negotiations collapsed. Oslo was not working, so I too needed to change my focus to be useful to the quest for peace with justice.

That ability to adapt personally and professionally is crucial, not just for me, but for anyone seeking sustainable change. It is true in matters of religious commitment as well, I have discovered – a not insignificant feature of the landscape, since Jerusalem is home to three faiths as well as two peoples. So I developed an understanding and appreciation for the different strands of Protestantism and Anglicanism, as well as the Orthodox and Catholic traditions that are 'closer to home' for me. Some of those Heads of Churches were my gurus in terms of advice but also of support. Similarly, inter-religious conversation and understanding is absolutely critical. Holding on to one's own convictions does not and should not mean dismissing those of others. Surprising moments of agreement and concurrence can and do occur, as well as the ability to handle differences and disagreements creatively, based on human contact and friendship across boundaries and borders. These are skills and aptitudes which I hope and believe I have absorbed deeply through my ecumenical endeavours. It is not a matter of 'lowest common denominator' thinking and action. There are higher common factors to be discovered and utilised, too.

So even when we are at loggerheads in explaining or appreciating the mysteries of faith, I am always able to go back to basics. I am not at all someone who is consciously pious or pietistic, as such outward manifestations feel counter-cultural to me, but the manifesto that guides me in biblical terms is Jesus's Sermon on the Mount, recorded variously in the Gospels of Matthew and Luke. This is a manifesto with profound personal and social implications – spiritually, politically, and yes, ecumenically. There is, for me, one God, manifested for us in the triune love of creation, the work of the spirit and the life, death, resurrection and ascension of Jesus Christ. We may and will have different ways of expressing humanity and divinity in Jesus, and so on. Across religions we will have even larger differences in the way we see God and Jesus. But when we serve God, when we seek to follow Jesus, we do so as human beings, whatever else can be said about us religiously, socially or culturally. It is in our humanity that we are bound together, and this humanity is God-given. That is also the message of the Sermon on the Mount. So, speaking personally, if I find Jesus in you, you are worth talking to and engaging positively, regardless of how you interpret Jesus. This is very important and central in my life.

Seeking common ground

There are, of course, many readers (and some friends or colleagues) who would be appalled by this "wishy-washy" and ecumenical approach. Fundamentalism is a disease within a whole variety of religious communities. It is, I believe, based on fear, and it can only be healed by an experience of the kind of unconditional acceptance which lies at the heart of God and the life of Christ. However, it is usually not religion that shifts people, but human interaction and the kind of political engagement which discovers a larger good at work in our relationships. Well, if there is a larger good at this level, it would be an even bigger good to learn to pray together – to discover our common dependence on God as the source and continuation of 'the good'. So that is what we are challenged to do, no matter how uncomfortable it might make us feel at first, and no matter that some will condemn and even oppose it.

This has a significant bearing on the diplomatic work I have been involved in, naturally. The Oslo process between the Israelis and Palestinians, facilitated in the past in an organisational sense by the Americans and involving a number of other parties such as the EU, the UN and Russia, was one I was engaging on behalf of a set of Christian communities. My role, as I saw it, was to help ensure that the Christian vision, contribution and input were not marginalised or watered down, but also that they were capable of engaging different perspectives and interests in a workable way. If you look at Jerusalem, the three faiths (Judaism, Islam and Christianity) live cheek by jowl. So during the process of political negotiations, what was worrying me was that the conversation could become one between Jews and Muslims, with the Christians left out. Yet the reality is that Christians have significant interests, not just demographically but in terms of their convents, monasteries, churches, hospitals and schools.

For example, at Camp David there was a crucial conversation about the Old City of Jerusalem, revolving around the fraught question about how its four Quarters – Muslim, Christian, Jewish and Armenian – might be divided. The idea was that the Christian and Muslim quarters would be under Palestinian Authority rule, whereas the Jewish and Armenian quarters would be under Israeli Government jurisdiction. This was unacceptable to most Armenians in Jerusalem, for many reasons – not just political ones, but because many Armenians would consider themselves strongly Palestinian as a matter of identity and upbringing, and this cannot simply be erased. Moreover, because the quarters are so close together, people could be living in one and working in another. To require Armenians to be divorced from their Palestinian reality would have severe implications for family life. It was a solution based on a theoretical equation, rather than lived reality – not dissimilar to the unfeasible way Arab countries were given frontiers and borders under Sykes Picot by the British and French. What is needed is a more relational and human approach. In this instance, I helped mobilise the churches to respond effectively to this challenge, and the outcome of our lobbying efforts was that Chairman Yasser Arafat, who was on the brink of considering the US-Israeli proposal understood the standpoint of all the churches and this idea was trashed – which of course did not help the negotiations.

Roots and routes

Bringing the story up-to-date, I have been working in recent years as a kind of freelance diplomat, ecumenist, lawyer or lobbyist and commentator. This has included a period of advising the Catholic Bishops' Conference of England and Wales on MENA and Gulf issues, continuing to assist the Armenian Church if and when necessary, working with ecumenical bodies and carrying out media duties within Britain and internationally. But more importantly, and while I earned my initial stripes from involvement with the Israel–Palestine challenge, my interests have broadened considerably since 2010 to include the whole MENA region as a follow-up to the 'Arab Spring' uprisings. As a lawyer, or perhaps as an individual, I have this "annoying" habit of trying to hold truth to power, and 'to say it as it is' – which is not how conventional politics are exercised and not always the way that church leaders express themselves too. The modest efforts that I deployed over the past decade sought to balance my deep concern about the Christian communities in the various countries of the region with the equal concern for the larger population that is Muslim in its majority. There is an urgent need to avoid falling into Christocentrism as one of the many *isms* that I dislike gutturally. The almost natural proclivity of some church leaders to defend oppressive regimes in the Arab World as a means of maintaining stability and thereby protecting their own Arab Christian communities is both dangerous and unwise. If anything, such attempts at courting the powers-to-be make the process of healing even harder. The issue, nevertheless, is how you tell the truth. It must be done in a way that enables people to face themselves and others honestly, not in a way that continues to wound or attack. This, I hope, has also been at the heart of my practice.

For that reason, I have also been pleased to work with academic institutions in France, the UK and beyond, to be an associate of the think-tank Ekklesia, and to pursue writing through the website *epektasis*. This website was in fact set up in late 1999, and has provided the substance of the material gathered in this volume. I have averaged an article a month over 19 years, having enjoyed more freedom to express myself of late, now that I am not answerable to higher authorities but can say what I think without fear or favour! That said, I continue to be conscious of the need to speak in a way that builds bridges rather than barriers, and which opens up new vistas of understanding a possibility (humanly, spiritually, politically) without endangering people and relationships in a fragile and often dangerous Israeli-Palestinian and wider MENA context.

The journey continues

I have no problem in accepting that I am in the twilight of my achieve-ments however I define 'twilight' or 'achievements'. Younger genera-tions must have their turn and their vision. They must make their own mistakes and adopt their own standpoints. So my hope is that the jour-ney described in this book will help and encourage those continuing to work for a just-peace in the region well beyond my own time and ca-pacity. The reflections that map this set of experiences are not those of a secular politician or of a church bureaucrat or an ordained minister, but of a person whose Christian faith remains central for him in a way that enables him to look at politics from the prism of faith and hope. Indeed, as the title suggests, I see the task as *keeping faith in hope* – the hope of a different and better future, a more fruitful political realign-ment, a diverse but common spiritual quest, and a renewed human spirit of understanding and enquiry.

But who am I *really*, you may still reasonably ask? Am I a politician? A churchman? A lawyer? A scholar? A diplomat? An analyst? A misfit even in an ever-changing world? But does it really matter? Perhaps the answer is that I am all of these and none of them exclusively. In fact, my favourite description is that I am a 'pessoptimist' taken from Emile Habibi's 1974 satirical fiction book entitled "The Secret Life of Saeed: The Pessoptimist. Otherwise put, I occupy an awkward but cre-ative space that is mine and that I facilely label as 'inter-disciplinary'. In Greek, *epektasis* (my website) is "stretching out" or "reaching out" This is what I have been seeking to do throughout my faith-based life. I have made mistakes, wronged people, disappointed friends, achieved some breakthroughs and highs as well as lows, been afraid and secure at the same time, got it right at times and wrong at others. In a nut-shell, I am just a very ordinary man whose ethnicity matters to him, whose faith is his companion, and whose "quests" have been journeys of learning as much as of teaching. And central to all this abides the Israeli-Palestinian conflict for me: it is a challenge to be won by well-meaning men and women in the face of Sisyphean odds.

This chapter has been created through conversation and cooperation between the author and the editor.

Part One: Enduring Conflict

Prologue

The first section of *Keeping Faith with Hope* examines the contours of conflict that have shaped the long and tragic history of Israel–Palestine since the Balfour Declaration was signed 102 years ago. The first chapter was written to mark that fateful anniversary. As the author avers, "[t]he 68-word text unleashed a chain of long-lasting repercussions that led to the eventual creation of the modern state of Israel in 1948." This was the genesis of a continuingly traumatic saga, not least for displaced Palestinians. Chapter two (first written in 2015) asks whether we should read the situation that unfolded from this founding dynamic as an inevitable or unalterable tale of woe. The biblical tradition of lament is one that involves recognising the symptoms and causes of pain and wounding, seeking sources of change in and through them via a process of rectification we call repentance. There is a flavour of that spiritually-driven realism and humanity in this material. Hope is not lost, but the foundations, politics and personification of enduring conflict must be faced. Chapter three therefore probes the idea and the reality of Palestine, the gap between the two, and the possibility of building bridges, while chapter four looks directly at the question of religion and politics – the competing claims of God and Caesar. Religion can be both a source of hope and just peacemaking, but also a distorted rationale or motivation for destruction. Again, these are issues we cannot duck or wish away. Lastly, in chapter five, the issue of fifty (plus) years of Occupation is dealt with directly. Recent events in Israel–Palestine illustrate a desire to ignore, minimise or melt away this fundamental injustice. But workers for justice and peace on all sides, and the international community as a whole, has kept us focus on the issue which above all needs resolution if the Land of the Holy One is truly to be a place of co-existence and flourishing for all one day.

Chapter 1

The Balfour declaration: a centenary of woes

The 2nd November 2017 marked one hundred years since the Balfour Declaration was made in a letter to the Jewish community in Britain. In a show of imperial diplomacy, that included these words:

> His Majesty's Government view with favour the establishment in Palestine of a national home for the Jewish people, and will use their best endeavours to facilitate the achievement of this object...

The 68-word text unleashed a chain of long-lasting repercussions that led to the eventual creation of the modern state of Israel in 1948.

Let me put aside the McMahon/Hussein correspondence (1915) that sought to win the allegiance of the Sharif of Mecca and his clan with offers of territory and power, or the Sykes-Picot agreement (1917) that carved up part of the Ottoman Empire between Britain and France. The 1917 Balfour Declaration (in Arabic, it is referred to as a 'promise') sought to create a pro-British bloc in Palestine but ended up being viewed by most Arabs as a calamity visited upon them.

A persistent gripe remains that while the declaration promised a "Jewish national home", it patently overlooked the fact that Palestine's "existing non-Jewish communities" – who incidentally were unnamed in the letter as the words Arab, Christian or Muslim were never penned down – made up some 90 per cent of the 700,000-strong population.

Hence, on the centenary of this declaration, the Balfour Project (UK), which includes clergy and laity alike, has been lobbying for a British formal apology to this historical misstep. The Declaration pledged Britain's support for a 'national home' for the Jewish people in Palestine on the understanding that the rights of 'existing non-Jewish communities in Palestine' would not be prejudiced either. The failure to uphold this second clause, for which Britain bore responsibility at the time, has fomented conflict between Palestinians and Israelis ever since.

In order to commemorate this event, we in the UK – and across much of the world – will witness myriad conferences and talks that push for one narrative or another as a consequence of this letter. Not only that, but a "festive" centennial dinner attended by Prime Ministers

Theresa May and Benyamin Netanyahu is on the menu too. I am among the many who believe that an unfortunate historical wrong was committed against Arabs in Palestine by this Declaration. It was motivated by Zionist ideology as much as by fundamentalist Christian thinking and political intrigues.

However, I do not support the campaign for a British "apology". For one, I do not believe HM Government will be forthcoming with such an apology that admits an historical impropriety. Perhaps coloured by my Armenian identity, I simply question whether the British Government would offer such an apology that rows back on its previous statements any more than the Turkish government would do so for Armenian genocide of 1915? Besides, I do not think it is politically expedient. Why not?

For well over three decades, I have argued strongly for Palestinian self-determination. Both before the now infamous Oslo process had inhaled its first breath, and long after it had exhaled its last, I maintained that Palestinians are owed their own sovereign, contiguous and secure state side-by-side with Israel. I also insisted that the West – and by that I do not mean only the USA but also the EU that have to date been bankers rather than politicians – owe it to Palestinians in both historical and ethical terms to help drag the parties toward a just and comprehensive resolution of the conflict.

However, I have also become aware that the political winds have shifted noticeably over the past decade. The once hopeful Arab Spring as much as the brutal counter-revolutionary reflexes in many countries, have moved global attention away from the remorseless woes of Palestine. The realignment of strategic alliances also means that Israel is no longer irretrievably the pariah for those Arab countries whose support is key to focusing global minds on Palestine.

Palestinians must instead request from the British Government a recognition of Palestine at the United Nations and across all international forums. The UK should push forward the long-overdue quest for Palestinian self-determination despite the irascible stonewalling of Israeli peace-unfriendly and colonial-friendly governments. Such recognition involves a firm commitment to peace with justice based on international legitimacy as well as equal rights for Israelis and Palestinians. It entails upholding International law, including the Geneva Conventions, without fear, favour or duplicity.

Much as this is a mammoth task and long-term challenge, I would suggest that it is a more pragmatic approach to the Palestinian stalemate and ultimately a more tangible output for Palestinians, too. But no British Government will necessarily undertake such recognition unless its citizens and politicians urge it to do so. Hence, a concerted lobbying effort is required by Palestinians and their British friends or allies. If Britain provides a lead, others will arguably follow suit.

Palestinians in 2017 are caught up in a Sisyphus-like scenario where they are patiently trying to push the boulder of apology up a steep mountain. But this is at best a frustrating and agonising exercise. Perhaps it is worth considering recognition as another option that draws them nearer to the fulfilment of the future – not only of the past.

30 October 2017

Chapter 2

Is it a tale of despair for Israel–Palestine?

Disagreements within the ruling coalition in Israel, particularly over the budget and a 'Jewish state' proposal, led to the dissolution of the government in December 2014. An election was held on 17 March 2015.

The incumbent Prime Minister, Benyamin Netanyahu of Likud, declared victory – though it took him until 6 May to put another coalition together. Hardly had the initial results from these Knesset elections been posted, than scores of pundits raced to pen down their opinions. It is always thus.

There were those who were jubilant, of course – in the USA, as well as in Europe and even within some ruling echelons of the Arab world. Then there were those who saw an apocalyptic cloud darkening further this land of milk and honey, perpetuating a fetid occupation and as a result strangling democracy.

In my opinion, the truth continues to lie somewhere between those two stark polarities. And that halfway grey zone exists whether Prime Minister Netanyahu denies the existence of a future Palestinian state or whether he accepts it with his mercurial qualifications.

I am frankly not bothered if Isaac Herzog was nerdy and lacked political charisma, or if Tzipi Livni cast a negative pall on the electorate. Nor do I wish to lampoon any of the other candidates, let alone address those grave domestic problems that the Zionist Union amplified almost exclusively – while Likud ignored them almost entirely, too.

At this moment I would merely like to argue why the outcome is not such an awful thing for the Israeli-Palestinian conflict. For someone who was involved with second-track negotiations during the Oslo years and who subsequently became disillusioned with this dud process, the re-election of Benyamin Netanyahu will magnify the sharply contrasting facets of the conflict and perhaps coerce the Palestinian Authority, the USA and the European Union to undertake some hard choices.

Regarding the Palestinian Authority. I am not an advocate of Hamas and I disagree with their ideology as much as I often do with their practices. However, I am nowadays also less of an advocate for a PA that has lost its way and sullied its early principles for the sake of maintaining the fiction of negotiations.

They have shuffled their positions continually in an attempt to keep the current *status quo* alive. It is surely time for them to examine this process a tad more openly and conclude that it has truly become an instrument that grants Israel all the geography it seeks for its illegal settlements, outposts or walls, fences and aquifers, whilst ridding itself of the human burden of the demography.

Is it not time to stop this charade, to dissolve the Palestinian Authority structures and to re-strengthen the PLO as the sole and legitimate representative of all Palestinians in the West Bank and Gaza? Would this not return the burden of occupation to Israel and kick in the apposite international conventions that carry legal obligations with them?

In terms of the USA, all we need to do to understand the weight of opinion and to realise the inequitable role that the country plays with regard to this conflict is to count the number of standing ovations for Prime Minister Netanyahu's address in front of the US Congress in Washington DC (twenty-six altogether), or witness the enthusiasm for the forthcoming visit by Republican House Speaker John Boehner to Israel to congratulate his ally.

Was it not the often-maligned Pat Buchanan who said to the McLaughlin Group in 1990 that "Capitol Hill is Israeli occupied territory"? Much as I respect those analysts who postulate that this might change due to the tensions between Obama and Netanyahu, I also disagree with them. The USA cannot become a fair arbiter, because doing so requires not a new man in the White House but a re-modelling both of the way many US politicians think and of the lobbying influence of pro-Israeli hard line organisations across the country.

In relation to the European Union – casting political pressure points aside, there is still so much economic muscle that this 28 state body can apply to help Israel comply with international legitimacy and end its 48-year-old occupation. After all, are the tariff reductions that Israeli goods enjoy under the EU-Israel Trade Agreement – an agreement which offers Israel more favourable treatment than any other country outside the EU – not conditional upon the respect of democratic and civil rights?

The EU has inexorably become a collective (or individual) banker with no credible say about the outcome of the conflict. From UK Prime

Minister Tony Blair as a failed peace envoy for the redundant Quartet, through to the phobia that Europe manifests when criticising Israel, has the EU become unprincipled, inept, inefficient and alas irrelevant?

The new Israeli coalition government will no doubt lurch the country toward more right-wing radical postures and in so doing alienate the slim prospects for a two-state solution. Prime Minister Netanyahu is not lying. The man speaks the truth when he says that he does not want a Palestinian state – Bar-Ilan notwithstanding – because he realises that one can barely be established on viable 1967 borders. Is this not the new political benchmark or are we lulling ourselves into a false inertia?

To my mind, the Israeli-Palestinian conflict remains one of the key hubs for the whole Middle East and North Africa (MENA) region. So given that the USA cannot contribute much on its own, and that Israel will simply continue to expand its colonies while fudging over the two-state solution, Palestinians should stand up for their rights. This requires bold steps rather than rhetorical fulminations – even if it means forsaking their 'privileges' – and the EU has to gird its loins (assuming it still possesses them) and act resolutely, too.

The Israel of sunny Tel Aviv is increasingly oblivious to the Palestinians' plight, and the Israel of sombre Jerusalem is vehemently set against any solution predicated on territorial compromise. So there can only be political motion once Israel feels the painful onus of occupation and when Israeli politicians like Stav Shiffer go head-to-head with the prevalent political practice of airbrushing Palestine out of the Israeli psyche.

Bite the bullet and move forward, I say, or else conditions will continue to fester, radicalism will be on the rise, and the tales of woe will lead to another conflagration. So I am not unhappy that PM Netanyahu was re-elected last week, but not for the obvious reasons. It may yet force various hands to move, rather than to allow the *status quo* to prevail. There is nothing inevitable or unalterable about the situation, unless the parties involved behave as if there is.

23 March 2015

Chapter 3

Palestine: an idea or a reality?

Looking at the Middle East and North Africa Region today, one cannot but be daunted by the colossal challenges facing its largely Arab inhabitants as they struggle to become full citizens in their own countries.

Syria, for instance, is bogged down in a low-intensity war that hapless United Nations monitors or spurious parliamentary elections will not resolve easily. In fact, the indescribably horrible explosions in the southern suburbs of the capital Damascus today [19 May 2012] are a sorry testimony to the implicit guilt and collective failure of the whole international community that has wantonly allowed the situation in Syria to run out of control and push the country into the spectre of a real civil war.

Egypt, on the other hand, is caught up in a tug-of-war between the Supreme Council of Armed Forces (SCAF) and Parliament over the future presidential elections, the nature of governmental coalitions, the fair principles of constitution drafting and the future of women's rights. Bahrain, not entirely different from Syria in some of its dynamics, shuts out the lessons of other Arab countries as it tries to quell any challenge to the authority of its rulers – whether by prisoners on hunger strike, by human rights' activists or demonstrators – with force and the ready help of Saudi Arabia or other Gulf countries. Yemen and Libya are also experiencing their own fault-lines with increasing tribal tensions and geographical polarisations whilst Tunisia is grappling with its fundamental freedoms and dispelling the opinion that it was the model revolution that set off the 'Arab Spring'.

Iraq, victim of an ill-considered invasion in 2003, is embroiled in a legal / political battle pitting the vice president Tariq Al-Hashimi against the prime minister Nouri Al-Maliki, and Jordan is experimenting with a rapid succession of pro-reform or reform-unfriendly governments. The phase of revolutions and counter-revolutions has firmly gripped this vast landmass and the jury is still very much out in terms of the verdict.

In fact, those revolutions and counter-revolutions have also drawn out the alignments and re-alignments that we have seen regionally – with the potential power-rooted landmines being anything from oil to religion. However, those long months of uprisings have not altered my immutable belief that they were not initially about politics or religion *per se* but much more about a sense of dignity that comes naturally with citizenship as well as with social and economic justice.

But in the midst of all those hobbling – and frankly less-than-tectonic – changes, where is the big elephant in part of the room? By that, I mean what has happened to Palestine, a virtual state clothed with a real idea, which had been at the forefront of the political imagination of the Arab masses for long decades?

It is quite clear that the multiple MENA uprisings across the region, the increasingly introverted political attitude of the Gulf Cooperation Council, the mesmerising and perilous standoff with Iran over the [non]-nuclear issue, the hawkish, 'I don't-give-a-damn' attitude of the present (and expanding) Israeli coalition government as it couples itself with a fragmented and negligent Palestinian Authority – all these factors have led to the gradual eroding of this reality of a Palestinian state, and have diluted its symbolic and emotional impact from the radars of many policy-makers or pundits.

However, much as we are all engaged in the different real uprisings in the region, pretending that the elephant is not in the room or is no more than an optical illusion – that is an exercise at self-deception which does not change the fact that this conflict which espouses one of the longest occupations in history, still remains a central hub for the peoples of this region. If it is not apparent today in the dust of so many 'revolutions', it will re-emerge with equal force soon.

The position of the Israeli-Palestinian conflict

So what can be said right now about the Israeli-Palestinian conflict? After all, the political inertia besetting this conflict remains steady despite all the dire warnings that the *status quo* is simply untenable. Even Tzipi Livni, the former leader of a once-hopeful Kadima party and deputy to former prime minister Ehud Olmert, suggested in her recent resignation speech that Israel was sitting "on a volcano", that "the international clock is ticking and the existence of Israel as a Jewish and democratic state is in danger" and that "for years, Israeli leaders have been burying their heads in the sand, occupying themselves with political exercises and spin and in that time the threat to Israel has only grown."

To put things in perspective, and to render the situation slightly less unreal in existential terms of struggle and suffering, it might be useful to recall that 1,600 Palestinian prisoners are on hunger strike today, with key names such as Thaer Halahleh, Bilal Diab or Jaffar Ezzedine grabbing our media headlines. Also, new illegal outposts, units or settlements on Palestinian lands are being systematically approved by the Netanyahu government, olive trees are being uprooted in West Bank towns such as Salfit and the boundaries of Jerusalem are relentlessly expanding (from 7,000 dunams / 1,730 acres in 1967 to 75,000 dunams / 18,500 acres in 2012) in order to accommodate further Israeli Jewish settlers. The Israeli twin political and ideological behemoths continue almost unhindered, whilst the US Administration strains to remain irrelevant and focuses solely on Iran as it prepares for its forthcoming elections. The world watches with rancid apathy.

Mind you, all this is happening when an Arab Peace Initiative that was approved by twenty-two Arab League member states in Beirut ten years ago lies on the negotiating table gathering diplomatic dust. Let us recall that this breakthrough initiative offered a comprehensive resolution to the Israeli-Palestinian conflict, the normalisation of relations between Israel and all its Arab neighbours and the possibility for a new dawn of regional stability and cooperation.

To illustrate the point, let me share one paragraph from a recent article by Dr Alon Ben-Meir, an Iraqi-born professor at New York University and an astute expert as well as regular writer on the Middle East:

> Whereas there is a constant stream of rhetoric about the desire to make peace with Palestinians, the Israeli government's actions on the ground belie its words. Instead of moving toward a solution to the Palestinian problem, Israel is taking steps that will jeopardize any hope of a peaceful settlement. The Netanyahu government's recent decision to retroactively legalize three West Bank settlements is nothing short of a shameless move that highlights the government's willingness to surrender to the whims of the settlement movement. Jerusalem's mayor, Nir Barkat, is promoting the establishment of a new settlement in East Jerusalem, a move that is bitterly antagonistic toward the Palestinians and threatens to diminish what little hope is left to forge a peace agreement which is sine qua non to Israel's own existence as an independent Jewish state. Out of desperation, the Palestinians may opt for a one state solution, which will force Israel to choose between being a bi-national state with a Palestinian majority in control or becoming an apartheid state earning international condemnation, increasing isolation, and eventually, crippling sanctions. Is this how the Netanyahu government tries to realize the Jews' millennium-old dream to live in security and peace?

With a reality that is almost unreachable and a virtual idea that is also becoming a smaller blip on our political screens, what can be done to ensure that this conflict is resolved so that Israelis and Palestinians live side-by-side in peace and security? One intuitive and disarming answer would suggest that we could have already been there if only Israel had agreed to pull out from the occupied territories in return for peace. When one recalls the Madrid conference, the protracted Oslo Accords with its Clinton Parameters, the Taba discussions, the Arab Peace Initiative, the Geneva Initiative, or grassroots projects such as One Voice, the formula has consistently been clear and constant: withdrawal from occupied territories in return for the full recognition of Israel and consequential overall peace.

A failed roadmap

But this formula has been found wanting. The roadmap that was endorsed and promoted by the Quartet has been an unmitigated disaster not only in terms of good will and good faith but also in terms of its dividends and results. Looking at the Palestinian and Israeli key protagonists, at the four constituent parties [the UN, the USA, the EU and the Russian Federation] or even at its peripatetic but largely inapt envoy Tony Blair, I maintain that this approach is sterile. In fact, a recent report by International Crisis Group entitled *The Emperor Has No Clothes: Palestinians and the End of the Peace Process* examines the real shortcomings of a process that was born in Oslo in 1993. The report suggests alternatives to what is widely recognised as a redundant process but one that helps Washington manage its relations with the Arab world and compensate for close ties to Israel. It also provides Europeans, Russians and the UN Secretary-General with a voice at a prestigious diplomatic table without any substantive *quid pro quo.*

In fact, all those sporadic peace talks that have been present by their sheer absence are simply meant to deflect international criticism and pressure from Israel. Besides, the Palestinians who suffer most from the *status quo* stand to lose if the comatose process finally were pronounced dead since the Palestinian Authority might well collapse and with it the economic and political benefits or favours it generates as well as the assistance it garners from different funders.

However, a lack of another irenic option does not justify the continuation of a doomed process that distinguishes itself with collective ineptitude and which also further marginalises the Palestinian grassroots' dreams for a sovereign and contiguous state. After all, everyone is liable – from the Palestinians who at times appear less concerned by Israel than they are by Gaza (and vice versa) to the other parties striving to perpetuate an illusion of momentum minus any real traction.

One part of the reason for such a stalemate is the parties' vested interests as much as tactical or political considerations. Another part is due to the fractious weakness of one party (Palestinians) and the fractious strength of the other party (Israel) who never fail to exert their mammoth lobbying prowess. Nonetheless, I would argue that it is still within the power of the parties to cobble together a just deal so long as all sides stop thinking about short-term gains but labour instead for long-term solutions. However, such a qualitative leap requires a firm vision that is alive and forward-looking, one that cannot alas be found today in the sort of political homunculi still clutching to power.

What of the future?
So what can the future hold for this small but hallowed plot of land that has been "blessed" by prophets old and new? In my view there will be no 'quick fix' to this conflict since none of the actors are truly ready to endorse a painful deal. Yet, the elements of a 'fix' remain painstakingly constant: the principles of international legitimacy, non-violent resistance to occupation, mass mobilisation, compromise from absolutist positions, cooperation rather than polarisation among Palestinians, closer integration and less hypocrisy among Arab states that have often used 'Palestine' as a panacea for their own ills.

But it is equally important for the West to conclude that its strategic interests point toward such a resolution and for the Israeli leaders to accept that the yoke of oppression they exercise with impunity upon Palestinians will eventually backfire and destroy the Jewish nature of the state and undermine its democratic values.

In a recent interview on *Al-Jazeera*, the celebrated artist Marcel Khalifé suggested that what is still lacking in the whole region is the sense of feeling free and then sharing that freedom with others. Are we not all very far off from that station of sharing freedoms, of dreaming, hoping and ultimately recognising the other in our own self?

19 May 2012

Chapter 4

Between God and Caesar

"Darkness is your candle
Your boundaries are your quest."
– M J Rumi (1207–1273), *Enough Words*

Imagine for one fleeting moment that you and your family are attending mass in your local church when a suicide bomber blows himself or herself up in front of you and in the process kills and maims members of your family as well as friends and acquaintances. Or that you are sitting at home when an anonymous message is surreptitiously dropped into the mailbox accusing you and your family of being infidels who should pack your bags and leave the country – your native country incidentally – or else face certain death.

How would you react to those two nightmarish situations or to other variations of those perils? How should the authorities of the country whose citizenship you enjoy also react in the face of such threats?

Alas, both those scenarios are not figments of an overactive imagination. They are sober realities [I am writing in 2011, but they echo down the years and across many countries] – the former in Egypt and the latter in Iraq – that are occurring with frightening frequency in the Middle East today. The outcome is a pervasive fear amongst some Middle Eastern Christians about their own physical safety, as well as an ulcerating unease over their sense of belonging to their own homelands or societies. Yet, simply by surfing the Internet, watching the news on television or listening to the radio, one can spot a rising tide of Christian-unfriendly militancy in regions as far apart as Pakistan and Iraq that is as much baffling as it is sinister. But why is this phenomenon rearing its ugly head these days, becoming dare I say a fashionable concern among many parties and leading to the disempowerment and emigration of vast numbers of indigenous Christians?

Multiple factors in the religion/politics matrix

I often also get asked why such phenomena occur much more in some Middle Eastern and North African countries than in others. Are they the product of war, conflict and chaos when the control of the state is weakened to the point where it compromises the rule of law? Or is it that some regimes manage to impose their rigorous laws much more successfully than others and co-opt Christians or other minorities as window-dressing in front of a supposedly enlightened and purportedly anxious West? Has it more to do with the political autism of the leaders in the region or even the mutating realignment of political forces? Is diversity a richness or a curse these days, and should it be nurtured and upheld or denigrated and even cleansed ethnically and politically?

There are obviously no easy answers to those questions, but rather numerous and often complex or even paradoxical reasons as to why such terrifying incidents appear to have become more frequent. And while it is well nigh impossible to go beyond the tip of the iceberg here, I would suggest that such cases are at times reminiscent of a *dhimmitude* (a French neologism that denoted initially an attitude of concession, surrender and appeasement towards Islamic demands, but that can also be summarised as the status of Jews and Christians as People of the Book under Islamic rule) that had dissipated from the region but that might now be whispering its timid return.

So let me try to identify a few of the culprits – contradictory culprits even – as they divert the course of a rational discourse that is steeped in the realities of the region and affecting its peoples, politics and faiths.

First, there is an abject absence of a real sense of Arab secular nationalism today; a tradition that had long enriched Arab societies in the past and to which Arab Christians had contributed strongly. Yet, this nationalism was a lodestar as much as a catalyst for cohesion in past decades until it was abused by the political regimes and powers-to-be within the Arab World or outside it and extinguished – though not necessarily expunged – from daily political realities. But this deletion created another vacuum in the world of 'isms' that has of late been replaced in part by the rigorous application of a Salafist-inspired and Wahabi-fed school of political Islam, whose ethos is a submissiveness that is exclusive of the other and propagates the principles of fire and brimstone rather than those of inclusiveness or commonality. This is the uncompromising mindset of many movements today, ranging from Yemen to Iraq and from Somalia to Afghanistan.

The brutal repression of fundamental freedoms alongside the quelling of dissent in many Middle Eastern countries – whether by power-hungry regimes, corrupt wheelers and dealers or big financial and corporate interests – have inexorably emasculated the Arab peoples and pushed them into a dark corner. In the past, those regimes had combated the creative ideas and freedom-seeking efforts of the intelligentsia within their societies by fomenting political Islamism as a diversionary and tactical counter-force; a force to distract the masses and then snuff out those tendencies seeking freedom, democracy and good governance. But what happened is that those religious movements then turned against the very dictators, autocrats and despots who were their original supporters. So recently we have been witnessing the confrontation and repression of ordinary peoples by secular politicians as much as by religious ones.

Moreover, there has been a parallel regression toward a brand of religious radicalism that is not only exclusive and insular but one that also blames the other for all the ills of society. This is at times perceptible within Islamist political movements such as Hamas or the Muslim Brotherhood that often use the double language of professing solidarity with those targeted Christians while also being susceptible to the anti-Christian aversion of their own populist bases that is sadly grounded on ignorance and prejudice.

Another factor lies in the skewered, hegemonic practices of some Western countries, whose own political and economic interests have led them to deal with those Arab countries and their masses as their serfs or as expendable commodities whose rights and resources can be used and abused for the higher interest of the colonisers. Despite all the expostulations of former British Prime Minister Tony Blair at the Chilcot inquiry, the invasion of Iraq is one appalling example of an ill-conceived policy that was not only illegal under International law but that also created chaos and made the local Christians appear as a fifth column in their own countries, simply because of their links with a universal – and mostly Western – Christian fellowship.

In fact, the deep irony here is that the West had previously often exploited those indigenous Christian communities and marginalised their importance. In all truth, it would even be useful to the foreign policy directions of some of our EU leaders and their allies if Arab Christians no longer stay in the region today so that the regional sectarian cleavages and confessional polarities that are at the very core of the conflicts in the Middle East become stark and consequently more manageable.

Then there is the lack of cogency in much of the Western argument, predicated on the notion that supporting Israel as well as oppressive secular regimes in the Arab and North African regions protects the West from the rise of a militant political Islam. True, political Islam can be limiting of many universal freedoms, but surely it is the very lack of fundamental freedoms and social opportunities going hand-in-hand with any oppression that eventually become the surrogate wombs procreating radicalism and even suicide bombers.

An inhospitable climate for Arab Christians

Next, we need to confront an inhospitable environment that alienates many Arab Christians from parts of the region and contributes at times toward blurring the sense of their identity – torn as they are between their deep sense of belonging, allegiance let alone love to the country of their birth and their legitimate desire to seek security as well as freedom, prosperity, welfare and happiness abroad – unaware that those promises of greener pastures often prove illusory and are not readily available elsewhere either.

Let us also not forget the sorry waste of potential arising from the mismanagement, corruption, contradictions or power-driven tugs-of-war within some churches, mosques or religious institutions. These bodies have failed to defend their communities effectively, and have therefore diluted – rather than strengthened – the bonds between the religious leaders or institutions and their peoples or even amongst communities within diverse societies. After all, much as numbers matter, is it not the quality of witness in any faith that helps distinguish it from sheer ideology?

Finally, consider the goal of movements such as *al-Qa'eda* in provoking a confrontation between the Arab world and the West. Such individuals, connected as they are through an idea or network rather than any Bin Laden-type central command, attack Arab Christians *inter alia* in order to stoke hatred and dissension, while also constantly radicalising their own base against all those Muslims and Christians who disagree with their neo-political beliefs or with their warped drive to control everyone else through terror, fear and subjugation. Yet in my understanding, and that of the great majority of believers worldwide, compulsion by religion is antithetical to the ethos of true faith.

Engaging cultural critique

Sadly enough, the Middle East today is struggling once more to re-mobilise a sense of *nahda* (renaissance) – whether intellectual, political or – across its ranks. Initiatives that can effectively challenge and inhabit the space currently occupied by a certain emptiness and listlessness. A recent book by Dr Elizabeth Kassab entitled *Contemporary Arab Thought: Cultural Critique in Comparative Perspective* (Columbia University Press, 2010) is erudite testimony to the fact that an enormous simmering potential of *hadatha* (modernisation) and *tanwir* (enlightenment) can be found amongst many Arab intellectuals today, but that it is being held back by those whose vested interests prefer oppression to democracy.

As such, instead of a revival in Arab thinking that would celebrate democracy, liberate society and then also – indirectly – incorporate and empower the Arab Christian communities, one lamentable outcome of such weighing factors is that many Middle Eastern and Arab-Muslim societies are now facing a vacuum that is being colonised by self-obsessed or self-important impostors; opportunist leaders who are seizing power for themselves and their causes, contributing toward a clash of religious or political ideologies and coercing the region into further intolerance and domination. Add the elements of poverty, unemployment and corruption to this lethal maelstrom and the Middle East becomes an angry tinderbox whose scapegoats also include irenic but disposable Christian communities.

Interestingly enough, what strikes me about the overthrow of the Tunisian president Zine el-Abidine Ben Ali on 14 January 2011 and the ongoing struggle against his Constitutional Democratic Party (a party, incidentally, that was neither constitutional nor democratic) is not so much the fact that an 'Arab Gdansk' or a 'Jasmine Revolution' has at long last taken root on the shores of an Arab-North African state. Rather, it is that this revolution is not commanded by political parties or central hubs but is a vibrant testimony to nascent Facebook and Twitter 'leaderless' generations who impelled Tunisians across all ages to go out and recover the dignity that they had been robbed of for over five decades. This is precisely why it might spread to other equally cobwebby states, albeit with unpredictable consequences.

But while a *vox populi* has impelled dramatic and hopefully lasting changes, there is also the obverse case of the rigged elections of 2009 in Iran, where repression held sway. Between Tunisia, Iran and the rest of the region, one can detect instances of religious totalitarianism no less nefarious than secular totalitarianism handcuffing progress, crushing dissent, muzzling the press and deriving their staying power from persecution.

Within those configurations, Middle East Christians remain an indispensable alloy in the fabric of Arab societies. Historically predating Islam, they have as much claim to the region as any other religion, ethnicity or dogma. They are co-equal citizens with their fellow Muslims – and with Jews in Israel and the occupied Palestinian lands – and it is high time that the authorities in all those countries assumed their responsibilities and celebrated such diversity by building them up rather than pressing them down, as well as protecting minority communities with the instruments of the law.

Hope or despair?

Am I painting a doom-laden scenario for Christians in the Middle East here? Yes and no. Yes, because the region as a whole stands on shifting sands. But also no, because I remain convinced that the overwhelming majority of ordinary Arab men and women of all persuasions – Christians, Sunnis, Shi'is, Kurds, Druze, Baha'is and others – are inherently decent people who simply wish to earn their daily bread, securely and peacefully. They are eager to co-exist with their neighbours. They are not genetic pariahs. Rather, it is the regimes themselves that muzzle and polarise their peoples, often aiding and abetting religious groupings into unhealthy political trade-offs. Did Lord Acton not famously remind us in a letter to Bishop Mandell Creighton in 1887, writing that "power corrupts, and absolute power corrupts absolutely"? This is a warning that has almost become a cliché, but which we still need to be reminded of again and again.

In this mix, it is a shame that ordinary citizens region-wide have not yet managed to find their voices in order to rise against unfaithful acts of power mongering. It is even a larger shame that a minority of patriarchal men are exerting every effort to muddy the waters and make the region unliveable for those who contest their agendas. Those violent men – be they from the Middle East or from the West – are propelled by hatred, self-interest, ignorance and misogyny and are patently antithetical to moderation, conviviality, and ultimately *ijtihad* and modernity.

This is why religious leaders in the Middle East should not shirk away from exerting every effort to educate their peoples to accept and respect the other, rather than to kill him or to ostracise her. They should have the raw courage – as did many ordinary Egyptian Muslims after the vicious attack on the Coptic Orthodox Church in Alexandria on 31 December 2010 – to stand up in solidarity with fellow Christians. But parallel to such a process of local education, our own religious leaders here in the West who often glibly bask in the dubious exercise of inter-religious fora, should also discern more astutely the tractions on the ground and stop pandering to those negative elements within MENA society, in the errant belief that everyone can become an inter-religious partner. Simply put, everyone cannot be a partner, and top-down dialogue or ecumenical and inter-faith handshakes are at times political ploys that do not deliver their intent but make the situation worse. After all, is this not what Jesus meant when he admonished his followers to turn the other cheek? Not to engage in power play, but to shame such actions.

Stark choices over religion and politics

In conclusion, much needs to be done to unpack the realities of the Middle East in terms of the interconnected and powerful matrices of politics and religion. Like the black widow spider devouring its host, politics and religion often feed upon each other in a relationship of mutually rewarding narcissisms. But one sign of hope for the future lies in decoupling those matrices and ensuring that future policies – or in some cases the lack of coherent policies – does not lead toward the inevitable displacement (by commission through encouragement, or by omission through compliance) of wholesale communities, something which is already being witnessed across the region today. Otherwise, the recent tragedies in Egypt and Iraq, let alone the unreported myriad incidents occurring elsewhere with unnoticeable regularity, will continue to metastasise and stealthily creep into other relatively more peaceful countries in the region too.

Do we wish for the kind of admixing of politics and religion in the Middle East that produces an incurably toxic hangover? Are we as a silent majority able and willing to stand up and be counted against the apocalyptic delusions and eschatological designs of the few? Or do we choose to run for cover? Our choices today could well determine not only our own futures but also the legacy we leave behind long after we have turned into dust ... again.

21 January 2011

Chapter 5

Fifty years of remorseless occupation

"All people are born free, and all people squirm for freedom." – Ben Ehrenreich,
The Way to the Spring

In June 2017 many Arabs commemorated the fiftieth anniversary of the Arab-Israeli Six Day War, a conflict that resulted in unmitigated disaster for the warring Arab nations of Egypt, Syria and Jordan. Spurred on by a false sense of pan-Arab nationalism that was rich in slogans and rhetoric but painfully wanting in weight or substance, all three Arab nations lost large chunks of territory. While 1948, and the creation of the State of Israel, was described by Arabs as their *nakba* (catastrophe), 1967 became their *naksa* (setback) and provided Israel the fulcrum of credibility for its future.

One consequence of this *naksa* is that Palestinians for the past fifty years have been seeking their own self-determination. They have been striving to build a proper state, with its sovereign trappings, on lands that were held by Jordan before the war in 1967. They have gone through multiple processes in order to incarnate their hopes. These have included terrorist attacks against Israel and other countries, followed by irenic initiatives (the most notorious being the Oslo process). But they have also settled in the last decade into a state of political torpor. Their ambitions for an independent state, living in peace next to Israel, were not made any easier by the fact that the world lost some of its concern for the Israeli-Palestinian conflict as a result of the Arab uprisings that erupted in 2010 and blazed across the Middle East and North Africa (MENA) region.

Geostrategic priorities

Since 2010, in fact, the geostrategic priorities of the Arab and world leaders have been far more focused on Syria, Iraq, Libya, Tunisia, and other countries rather than on the likelihood of a puny Palestinian state rising sphinx-like from the ashes of 1948 and later 1967. Palestinian deep divisions and internecine squabbles have not facilitated this dream either. Nor have the illegal settlements that have voraciously spread their predatory tentacles across much of East (Arab) Jerusalem and the West Bank. Or the segregation wall that has perhaps reduced attacks on Israel but has in the process caged a whole people collectively behind barbed wires and concrete blocks. Even travelling from one Palestinian village to another within autonomous areas is a chore. So how can one detect any sign of hope given those dire straits?

Freedom and dignity is the essence

As someone who earned his initial stripes on the platform of the Israeli-Palestinian conflict, but who somewhat took his eye off the ball for a while to focus on the wider MENA region, I decided a few weeks ago to plunge into some fresh reading on the narrative of Palestinians and Israelis. I did not choose to peruse some of the recent learned opinions and sophisticated papers of academics, experts or officials. Instead, almost counter-intuitively, I chose instead books and articles whose authors would refresh my mind on a Palestinian cause that seeks peace with justice.

One book that particularly struck me was Ben Ehrenreich's *The Way to the Spring*. It is the unvarnished account of the author's journalistic experiences in Nabi Saleh (northwest of Ramallah, in the occupied West Bank) and the painful suffering of Palestinian men and women struggling tirelessly for their breath of freedom. I was also drawn to an article by Sarah Yerkes, Fellow at Carnegie Middle East Programme, who expressed the hope that the young boys and girls of this conflict might conquer their fear and find hope in the next fifty years. But honestly, another fifty years of injustice, stasis, disenfranchisement and pain?

Wading through various books and articles, I realised once more that the Israeli-Palestinian conflict, in its essence, is a case of a people seeking basic freedom and dignity, as well as the right to found a state. Palestinians seek to unshackle external domination and build their lives for themselves. I am of course aware that Palestinians and Israelis alike have besmirched their histories with wars, massacres, betrayals, abuse of power, religious bigotry, scandals and blatant crimes against human rights. I also understand why they both distrust each other and perceive that they are struggling for an existence that simply cannot include the other side. Alas, this is a sad and persistent lose-lose scenario. It is precisely this that we have to move away from.

Statehood and an unequal struggle

But I also realise that all the language I have just used is not the actual way that countless ordinary Israelis and Palestinians perceive the conflict. What is key for each of them is an aspiration to have a state they can call home. They refuse a remorseless occupation that has, as of 2017, lasted fifty years; one that coerces, abuses, separates and de-institutionalises their rights.

Palestinians were given a bad hand from the start when the British Mandate betrayed them. But they were also betrayed time and again by many Arab leaders who callously used the Palestinian cause as a fig leaf for their own interests. They have been considered no more than pawns on a chessboard-- expendable for the sake of the more precious pieces. But the Palestinian resilient strength is that they have not forsaken their dream for political redemption over half a century. Moreover, the Arab and Muslim peoples still defend the justice of their cause.

This is what fifty years mean to me: an unequal fight between a David fending off the many Goliaths gnawing at its rights. Or perhaps even a Sisyphean task against powers and principalities that strive to keep Palestinians stateless and stunt their legitimate hopes for self-determination. Yet, I see the courage of this people and I raise my hat again to them today.

11 June 2017

Part Two: Negotiating Hope

Prologue

In December 2017, US President Donald Trump defied overwhelming global opposition by recognising Jerusalem as the capital of Israel, insisting that the highly controversial move would not derail his own administration's bid to resolve the Israeli-Palestinian conflict. In this section the background to Jerusalem as a shared and contested space crucial to the future of region is considered (chapter six), by looking back at the ever-present issue from the vantage point of 2001. The Oslo process is one that has occupied the author, and vast tranches of commentary on the Israel–Palestine question, for many years. Oslo is touched on in more detail in the book's introductory chapter, 'Travelling in Hope', and the afterword, 'Hope Revisited'. That frees up this section on negotiating hope to look at two other features of the recent terrain – the 2007 Annapolis conference (chapter seven), and the often-overlooked relationship of Palestinians and Kurds (covered in chapter nine). In the meantime, chapter eight (from 2005) looks at the occupied territories of Gaza and the West Bank, the challenging issues of geography and demography, and the 'narrow gate to peace'. Last but not least, chapter ten brings us up to date on the latest claims of a 'deal of a century', the unforgiving realities that underlie deal-making given the current political hegemony, and the damaging impact of a sharp change in US policy under Trump.

Chapter 6

Palestinians and Israelis ... in Jerusalem?

Introduction

Jerusalem – known in Arabic as *al-Quds* and in Hebrew as *Yerushalaim* – is meant to be a city of sacredness and peace. It is also a city of two peoples and three faiths bound together by history and destiny on a small parcel of land. But this picture of pluralism and diversity, of peace and holiness, is being constantly challenged by two different conceptions and realities.

Indeed, as a city sacred in equal measure to Jews, Christians and Muslims, God is being held hostage to the interests of men. Men and women are also being held hostage to their own whims. As a city whose name calls for peace, victimhood and victimisation have nonetheless become the normative currencies of this city, let alone of the West Bank and Gaza as a whole.

In this small land, where God chose to reveal the divine will, Israelis and Palestinians are at war. Living side-by-side, erstwhile historical neighbours and peace partners are now fighting each other. Pisgat Ze'ev and Beit Hanina, Gilo and Beit Jala, Psagot and Ramallah, Netzarim or Kfar Darom and Gaza. Neighbourhood against neighbourhood, Jewish settlement against Palestinian town, the violence that is deadly, bloody and unjust continues unabated to date.

Policies of contradiction

Israel claims that Jerusalem – the whole city with its eastern and western sectors – is the eternal and undivided capital of Israel. Palestinians, on the other hand, stress that West Jerusalem can only become the capital of Israel so long as East Jerusalem can become the capital of Palestine.

This a straightforward contradiction. Semantics do not substitute for the reality on the ground. Anyone who is familiar with Jerusalem knows that there is a clear psychological separation between the western (Jewish) and eastern (Palestinian) sectors of this city. This division straddles clearly the few hundred yards between two of the seven gates of Jerusalem – Damascus Gate and New Gate.

The walled old city of Jerusalem has four quarters that still exist today. They are the Armenian, Christian, Jewish and Muslim quarters. Between them, they house the majority of those sites that are holy to the followers of the three monotheistic traditions.

Another contradiction. Instead of lifting up the religious character of this small city, Israel and the Palestinians are fighting over political sovereignty. Power and control are the ingredients that describe this small sacred space which is meant to move beyond such temporal struggles.

Israel constantly reminds the world community that it can never relinquish its hold over Jerusalem. A people who spent long years in exile seeking to return to their spiritual home will not give up a city that once held the Temple and housed the Ark of the Covenant.

More contradiction. Much as Jerusalem is irrefutably sacred to Jews, it is sacred in equal measure to Muslims and Christians worldwide. Much as Israel cannot give it way, nor can the Christian and Muslim worlds. Besides, why does Israel interpret the religious significance of Jerusalem through a political lens that insists upon sole *de jure* and *de facto* control of the whole city?

Unilateral measures

Given this reality, and in view of the fact that the whole process of political negotiations now taking place is over a mere 22 per cent of historical Palestine, it is regrettable that Israel is using a variety of measures to alter the demographic make-up of this small percentage of land under negotiation. Measures employed by Israel include, *inter alia*, the following.

First, revocation of residency rights for scores of Palestinians from Jerusalem who may have lived outside the city or abroad for a number of years – due to studies, employment or marriage. In pursuing this discriminate policy, the Israeli Ministry of Interior is overlooking the fact that those residents were born in Jerusalem. It is also making a frightening contrast in its attitude toward Jews who have an automatic 'right of return' to Israel, whereas Palestinians do not, regardless of their birthrights.

Second, although 90 per cent of unlicensed houses are built in West (Israeli) Jerusalem, only 10 per cent of those are demolished by the municipality. Of the remaining 10 per cent built in East (Arab) Jerusalem, 90 per cent are nonetheless systematically demolished by the municipality (Jeff Halper, Alternative Information Centre – AIC statistics).

Third, a massive settlement drive in Jerusalem and the West Bank is altering the geo-demographic makeup of this land and establishing obstacles to peace on the ground. One consequence of this settlement drive is that wholesale Palestinian town and villages are being sieged or encircled, and territorial contiguity between Palestinian areas is no longer viable or possible.

Fourth, Israeli closures of the territories continue, and the northern and southern sectors of the West Bank are cut off from Jerusalem with hardly any flow of goods or movement of persons.

A psychology of peace or war?

It is true that Israelis are fearful for their cultural, religious or historical identities. This fear within the Israeli Jewish psyche is legitimate and ought not be dismissed summarily. It is also in another part an inevitable unfolding of history. Yet, Palestinians have legitimate rights too, and resistance to such rights by either side tots up the pain and losses on both sides.

Israel is fully within its right to exist with security in the Middle East. However, it cannot use its overwhelming military might to coerce another people into submission and surrender. It cannot simply pretend that well over three million Palestinian men and women do not exist on Palestinian soil. Israeli security relies largely upon a peace agreement with its Palestinian (and Arab) neighbours that recognises the principles of international legality enshrined in the United Nations Security Council (UNSC) resolutions and associated international covenants or agreements.

Instead of mutual negation and mutual recrimination, what should be strengthened today are goodwill, good faith and mutual trust. They alone can lead to the confidence-building measures that provide a win-win solution for both peoples and possibly lead toward ultimate reconciliation. Such a peace alone can revoke the radicalism – religious and political – that is besetting this region and taking it down the spiralling path toward further violence.

This outcome is a responsibility that Israelis and Palestinians must assume with courage. But it is one that the European Union – as a political body – and the international NGO's – as a moral force – should also pursue with relentless vigour, clear advocacy and targeted lobbying.

The challenge of Jerusalem is considerable, and in that context the future of the region looks gloomy. Israel will remain an invincible and unconquerable military giant in the midst of a weak and riven Arab world. Its economy will be stronger than those of most of its Arab neighbours. But it will still have no genuine and lasting peace. Its security will remain threatened, exposed and false. The suffering and bereavement of Palestinians and Israelis destined to live together could well continue much longer.

Unless, of course, there is peace ... ?

3 April 2001

Chapter 7

The Annapolis Conference

According to my handbook, Annapolis is a city located in central Maryland on the south bank of the Severn River, near the mouth of the Chesapeake Bay. It celebrates this year [2007] *Annapolis Alive!* which consists of a yearlong series of events sparked by the 300th anniversary of the signing of its Royal Charter and the marking of its independence and participatory democracy. However, what my manual does not add is that this city will host on 27 November a conference at the US Naval Academy that brings together Israelis and Palestinians, along with a number of Arab states as well as the Quartet, the G-8 and smaller players such as Norway, Turkey and Senegal. Together, they will discuss the issues that pertain to the creation of an independent Palestinian state.

A multivalent conversation

One question is to determine the countries that will finally join Israel and the Palestinians round the table of negotiations. For instance, it would be important to include high-level Jordanian and Egyptian participation since those are the only two Arab states that have diplomatic relations with Israel. It is equally important to have Saudi Arabia at Annapolis, not least because the kingdom chairs the Arab League committee promoting the 2002 Arab peace initiative and its presence is a buy-in for larger Arab support. Syria, on the other hand, has been ambivalent about its participation and has stressed that it is conditional upon discussing the return of the occupied Golan Heights.

In fact, HM King Abdullah II of Jordan visited Syrian President Bashar El-Assad in Damascus last weekend to discuss the prospects for Annapolis, in addition to the Lebanese presidential crisis, Iraq and other regional concerns. To date, the only near certainty seems to be the attendance of the two main protagonists – Israel and the Palestinians – whose number of handshakes between their leaders belies the ostensible progress made between them as well as the four Members of the international Quartet.

Indeed, the newly appointed envoy for the Quartet, British ex-Prime Minister Tony Blair, who has been ensconced in his base of operations at the American Colony Hotel in Jerusalem, has been grappling with his job of unveiling a host of economic incentives and helping found a functional Palestinian state. It is therefore hoped that his international staff of 14 and an $8 million first-year budget would unwrap the Quartet from its stale packing and help broker such a historic deal.

One main reason why it took so long to set a date for the now-one-day conference is that the Palestinian and Israeli committees have not yet managed to finalise a concrete document that is tantamount to a declaration of principles for peace, and their efforts have continually been downgraded from the initial and ambitious framework for a comprehensive peace deal-- so much so that the objectives of both parties have become somewhat distant and incompatible with the original hype that accompanied the idea of Annapolis when it was first introduced by the US Secretary of State.

Am I being a tad too harsh? Last week, the Palestinian Independent Commission for Citizens Rights, documenting Israeli restrictions on Palestinians, stated that most Palestinians living in the West Bank share a strong sense of scepticism. Their spokesperson added that US Secretary of State Condoleezza Rice has made seven trips to the region this year, but restrictions on Palestinians in the West Bank in the form of roadblocks and checkpoints have become even worse. Moreover, the Palestinian political analyst, Hani al-Masri, said that the pressure is now on the Palestinian side to return from Annapolis with real concessions from the Israelis-- something few Palestinians believe will happen during this event. So what happens at Annapolis, who has a say in the outcome, and what pitfalls need to be avoided to ensure some momentum that draws the conference away from the brink of a fiasco?

Weakened negotiators

I am afraid I do not see anything that is hugely different today from the realities prevailing during the final status talks that broke down in 2001 amidst mutual recriminations and the start-up of another Palestinian Intifada. To start with, it is clear to me that Israeli PM Ehud Olmert is a weakened premier who is making courageous noises about broad peace whilst also warning all and sundry not to augment the level of expectations about any major breakthroughs.

In fact, and not unlike other Israeli leaders before him, it seems to me that the current prime minister might also be much more interested in perpetuating a peace process that hobbles on for more years than he is interested in a real and durable peace between both sides on the basis of national rights, security and justice that requires painful sacrifices. This might be as much because of a reluctance to give up territory as it is by the fact that his own shaky coalition would fall like a pack of dominoes in case he makes any substantive gestures toward the Palestinian side or even that he is himself under criminal investigations.

Palestinian Authority President Mahmoud Abbas, on the other end of the irenic spectrum, is an equally weak negotiator. After all, part of the Palestinian territories [the Gaza Strip] is not under his control, whilst the other parts [the West Bank] could slip out from under him too despite the increasing unpopularity of Hamas and the massive injections of funds by donors into cities like Nablus in the northern West Bank. In fact, the latest aid to Nablus by the US Administration – amounting to an admittedly modest sum of $1 million – is meant to fund projects in this restive city of 200,000 Palestinians and give it a facelift that would help with the ongoing "hearts and minds" popularity campaign.

But what renders the Palestinian credibility thinner are the absence and clear opposition of Hamas. Regardless of its defiant and unfriendly ideologies, hard-line policies or adversarial positions, I fear that the total marginalisation of Hamas from the current Palestinian political landscape could render more complex any future negotiations. No wonder that many Palestinian grassroots organisations are calling for direct elections to the Palestine National Council (PNC) and the reactivation and democratic reform of the PLO institutions that have become either too otiose or too nepotistic.

But let us for one moment forget that both sides are unable, or worse unwilling, to sue for peace. Let us also dismiss the reality that their objectives are divergent, with PM Olmert preferring a broad-brush non-binding joint statement whilst President Abbas pursuing a detailed framework agreement with a timeline for final-status negotiations. The fact remains that the issues surrounding a nascent Palestine are still as cumbersome and insuperable as ever.

Facing the challenges

For Annapolis to become different from its moribund predecessor conferences, summits and pow-wows, it is imperative not only to discuss final status issues but also to act upon them in a decisive manner that delivers palpable and concrete results. Those issues that need to be hammered out include land, borders and territorial withdrawals (which would also deal with new and expanding settlements with well over 200,000 settlers, let alone the parameters of the separation wall), the future of Jerusalem (including the Old City that hosts many religious sites precious to Jews, Christians and Muslims alike), water, security guarantees for both sides and refugees. However, what remains the hardest nut to crack is the matter of the over four million Palestinian refugees who would wish to see an implementation of the Right of Return.

Would it be possible for the two sides – even with the help of the Quartet – to tailor any deal that comes near enough to tackling those issues and delivering upon them? Are there the will and vision to find solutions to unfriendly problems? Equally importantly, where is the good will to move forward, and where is the good faith to show compromise wherever necessary in order to overcome obstacles? Only this week, Palestinian chief negotiator Ahmad Qrei and his team tried to enter Jerusalem from the Abu Dis district in order to meet with their Israeli counterparts and to discuss the Annapolis agenda. However, they were stopped at the checkpoint that straddles the 25-foot-high-wall and the meeting was axed eventually. It took Israeli Foreign Minister Tzipi Livni to call Qrei and apologise for this administrative [security] hiccup. It is true that this might be a simple enough incident, but it just shows the steepness of the mountain of mistrust on both sides if a chief negotiator cannot move into Jerusalem freely for pre-arranged negotiations with his Israeli counterparts!

In numerous articles in the past, I have advocated that one signal way forward is for Israel to accept the Arab / Saudi offer made at the Arab Summit of 2002 that traded full withdrawal from occupied territories by Israel with recognition of Israel by all Arab states. Alas, successive Israeli political establishments have not yet endorsed this offer. Perhaps it is time to do so now, especially if the incumbent US Administration has finally woken up to the fact that it had been dangerously somnolent for the past seven years in relation the Israeli-Palestinian conflict.

Hope or scepticism?

So will this latest Annapolis conference – or more to the point this "one-day meeting" since it has been downgraded from a "two-day conference" – succeed where others failed, or have we not yet reached the classical peak of the bloody conflict to start talking about real resolutions? To be successful, Annapolis needs a genuine commitment by the US Administration, but I doubt the USA will import such a laborious commitment into this process. Rather, I think that this whole meeting could end up as another public relations effort or a photo-op that strives to show momentum, willingness and determination to move ahead on the Israeli-Palestinian file at a time when the American reputation is sadly smeared in the majority of the Arab and Muslim worlds.

However, what unsettles me even more is that this meeting could merely become a way to build an alliance with other so-called moderate Arab states against Iran's increasing hegemonic strength. Or as Martin Indyk from the Saban Center at the Brookings Institution said recently, it is an attempt at building "an anti-Iran counter-alliance". Yet, if the USA were to fail in its latest endeavours to forge this very alliance, then it is quite possible that many of the Arab states would reconsider their tactical plans and perhaps try to win Syria over again by offering it the carrot of re-entering Lebanon. The US Administration would then face a Faustian bargain that would imply continuing the struggle against Iran at the cost of its own oft-stated principles.

A new verb, *lecondel,* has entered colloquial usage in Hebrew. Based upon the name of US Secretary of State Condoleeza Rice, it signifies 'to come and go for meetings that produce few results'. So what is Annapolis, in Maryland, all about? Is it about peace? Is it about Syria and Iran? Is it another ripple in the murky pond of Middle Eastern politics? Will it be any more successful than Camp David was under Messrs Clinton, Arafat and Barak? I am painfully concerned that, once bereft of the frills, hype and verbiage, Annapolis will also become another one-day meeting where scepticism overtakes hopes – and in the process disappoints the laudable efforts of countless Palestinian and Israeli peace-seekers.

22 November 2007

Chapter 8

From Gaza to the West Bank

"A Jew does not expel a Jew, he just moves him a little bit." – sticker on car bumpers in Israel, August 2005

Israel seems to be in turmoil these days, as an emotional tug-of-war is being waged by a relatively small number of settlers against the decision by the Israeli Government to 'disengage' from all the settlements in the Gaza Strip and from 4 small and isolated outposts in the northern West Bank. In fact, the graffiti on the walls hector PM Ariel Sharon for his decision to pull out from Gaza, and one of the more populist writings that 'a Jew does not expel a Jew' repeats the dramatic words of nineteen-year-old Cpl Avi Bieber that became the slogan for the pro-settler movement.

Indeed, the air is not only replete with ominous warnings and declarations that go so far as to compare the fate of Israelis today with those during the Second World War in Poland, but pro-pullout and anti-pullout ribbons are also being distributed across Israel. Those in favour of the pullout hand out blue ribbons that represent the colour of Israel's flag, while those opposing the pullout hand out bright orange ribbons as the colour of their struggle.

Even a senior cabinet minister walked away from the notion of collective responsibility, when Benyamin Netanyahu submitted on 7 August 2005 his resignation as Minister of Finance in protest against the withdrawal from Gaza. However, Ehud Olmert quickly replaced Netanyahu, and the polls suggest that nearly half of the Israeli population believe the resignation was motivated by an attempt to undermine Ariel Sharon's leadership of Likud in the forthcoming primaries and to pave the way for the next general election.

So, given such breaking news and grabbing headlines in Israel and the Occupied Palestinian Territories, one would probably be forgiven for thinking that this huge upheaval is due to a total Israeli pullout from all territories it occupied during the Six-Day War of 1967, and that all the settlers on occupied lands are being evicted from their settlements. After all, 55,000 Israeli soldiers are meant to guarantee that the pullout takes place according to plan.

In fact, things are somewhat different since we are referring only to an Israeli withdrawal from 21 settlements in the Gaza Strip that house less than 9,000 settlers and from Sa Nur, Homesh, Kadim and Ganim in the West Bank that were established in the early 1980s and that together have no more than 600 settlers living in them. Indeed, as Diana Buttu, legal adviser to the Palestinian Negotiating Support Unit underlined in a television interview last weekend, the overall pullout only affects one per cent of Palestinian occupied territories and two per cent of settlers on Palestinian land.

Geography and demography

One quick look at the map of the Gaza Strip provides a graphic idea of how geography and demography are overlapping in this settlement-led conflict. The 15 settlements in southern Gaza, known as the Gush Katif, account for the bulk of the settlers, whilst the remaining six are toward the northern and central parts of this strip of land. Of those, a large number of settlers, and the majority of the Israeli population, are reconciled to varying degrees with the inevitable need to move out of the settlements. However, the settlements of Kfar Darom, Morag, Netzarim (established in the early 1970s, with roughly 1,200 inhabit-ants) as well as that of Shirat Hayam (established in 2000, with merely 40 settlers) are the most devoutly religious and ideological ones. They have been causing a large degree of the polarisation within Israel.

I believe that the recent developments predicate a number of salient points. An Israeli government (and no less a hawkish one than a Likud-led one headed by Ariel Sharon) has established the principle of withdrawal from occupied territories. This precedent should be welcomed let alone invoked as a precedent in the future. Moreover, it does not mean that Israel could use Gaza as its backyard to go in whenever it perceives an incursion necessary-– irrespective of any deference to sovereignty, custom or circumstance.

The Palestinian factions should avoid any attacks on Israel, let alone any fratricidal struggles, and prove instead to the world that they are both willing and able to govern their lands. Any in-fighting and blood-shed would play into the hands of those who insist that Palestinians simply cannot govern a state and are more inebriated with the idea of freedom than with exercising good governance and states-like respon-sibility. Today, a cessation of violence remains an American sine qua non for further Israeli concessions, and this ramps up the burden on the Palestinian Authority – led by its President Mahmoud Abbas – to take effective control of those unchained territories in Gaza.

This phase of withdrawal could only be the stepping-stone – not the culmination – of the process of peace. Israel should not be allowed to consolidate its settlements in the West Bank, and the Israeli hard-line thesis that by 'giving' President Bush Gaza, Israel will have bought for itself at least a lack of American pressure so that it can annex the West Bank, should be disproven rapidly. After all, the rusty Roadmap for Peace calls for Israel to work with elected Palestinian officials for a negotiated Israeli withdrawal from the West Bank and Gaza.

Admittedly, it is the duty of the Palestinian Authority to ensure that it clamps down on terrorism and violence against Israel, but it is equally the duty of Israel – and by proxy that of the otiose Quartet – to ensure that Palestinian statehood does not slip off the agenda indefinitely. As I see it, this withdrawal is a precursor for an Israeli withdrawal from those settlements in the West Bank that are not already *de facto* parts of Israel, and subsequently for the creation of an independent and viable Palestinian state.

Gaza cannot become a cage for gaoling over 1.2 million Palestinians. There are seven crossings between Gaza and Israel that could provide lifelines for the economic survival of Gaza. Besides, Palestinians should be allowed access to their borders and coastline, territorial waters and airspace-- not be controlled, *manu militari,* by Israel.

The Palestinians should also take this opportunity of regaining their land to improve the situation of the Palestinians still resident in refugee camps. Those camps are a painful reminder of a dispossessed and scattered people, but they are also showpieces against occupation, and should now be developed further with assistance from the European Union.

In the midst of all those political permutations about the withdrawal from Gaza and future withdrawals from the West Bank, it should not be forgotten either that Israel is also solidifying its hold over a wide area in and around the city of Jerusalem, creating a far broader city and gradually destroying the pragmatic tools that would lead to a viable two-state solution.

It is in fact implementing a focused and systematic plan that, if carried out, risks choking off Arab East Jerusalem by further fragmenting it and surrounding it with Jewish settlements / neighbourhoods. As the International Crisis Group (ICG) observed in its Executive Summary and Recommendations entitled *The Jerusalem Powder Keg,* there are grim concerns over Jerusalem.

The separation barrier, once completed, would create a broad

Jerusalem area encompassing virtually all of municipal Jerusalem as expanded and annexed in 1967 as well as major settlements to its north, east, and south. This new 'Jerusalem envelope', as the area inside the barrier euphemistically has been called, incorporates large settlement blocks and buffer zones, encompasses over four per cent of the West Bank, absorbs many Palestinians outside of municipal Jerusalem and excludes over 50,000 within, often cutting Palestinians off from their agricultural land.

Expansion of the large Ma'ale Adumim settlement to the east of Jerusalem and linking it to the city through the E1, a planned built-up urban land bridge, would go close to cutting the West Bank in two.

New Jewish neighbourhoods and settlements at the perimeter of the municipal boundaries would create a Jewish belt around Arab East Jerusalem, cutting it off from the West Bank and constricting Palestinian growth within the city.

The shifting physical and political landscapes in Israel and Palestine today would suggest that Israel has 'won this round'. After all, it seems that Ariel Sharon has almost fulfilled Menachem Begin's advice to ensure permanent Israeli control over the entire 'Land of Israel' whilst foreclosing the emergence of a viable Palestinian state. If this were the case, it is important to re-energise the now-somnolent international civil society.

The narrow gate to peace

Jeff Halper, an Israeli anthropologist and coordinator of the Israeli Committee Against House Demolitions, writes in 'The Narrow Gate to Peace' (*Sojourners,* August 2005) that, "the people, gathered into hundreds of organisations worldwide that support Palestinian rights – faith-based communities, human rights organisations, political groups, trade unions, Israeli and Jewish peace groups, Muslims, Christians, intellectuals, students, unaffiliated members of the public – have at their disposal a growing awareness of the importance of human rights and instruments of international law." He stresses that those civil forces should demand the end of the occupation and the right of Palestinians to self-determination through non-violent measures of protest, resistance and international sanctions such as divestment.

As Meron Rapaport argues in *Le Monde Diplomatique,* the withdrawal from Gaza should *prima facie* lead both parties to re-address the issues of the West Bank where Palestinians are increasingly being locked into 70 walled enclaves, and where over 240,000 Israelis live in

200 settlements. As a press briefing from the Council for British-Arab Understanding elicits, Israel today is preparing 50 other West Bank settlements, planning to build 6,391 new housing units and 'legitimising' another 120 unauthorised settlement outposts.

If the international civil society does not assume its obligations but rather forfeits its struggle against occupation, then the less-than-opaque prediction uttered by Dov Weisglass, senior adviser to PM Ariel Sharon, that the disengagement from Gaza is solely the formaldehyde that would put to sleep the political process with the Palestinians could well and truly become a sobering reality. If so, the ensuing implosions would render the whole region increasingly more unstable, radical, bellicose and ultimately dangerous.

16 August 2005

Chapter 9

Two peoples, two hopes, two futures

In April 2009, Mahmoud Abbas, President of the Palestinian Authority, flew to Irbil in Kurdistan from Ramallah in Palestine and met with Massud Barzani, leader of the Kurdish regional government. According to various news dispatches, the visit aimed at centring the ties between the two largest stateless peoples in the Middle East. In fact, this trip also came one week after Abbas had held talks with Iraqi President Jalal Talabani, in Baghdad, in what was the first visit to Iraq by a Palestinian leader since the 2003 US-led invasion that ousted Saddam Hussein.

Two visits, two issues
Looking at it from an EU prism, and putting aside the lavish praise that was exchanged between guests and hosts on both occasions, there are two distinct but inter-related issues that flow out of those two simultaneous visits.

The first issue is the pressing if somewhat overdue concern of the Palestinian Authority for the fate of Palestinians in Iraq. According to Daniel Endres, the Swiss head of the Iraq office of the United Nations High Commissioner for Refugees (UNHCR), there were roughly 60,000 Palestinians living Iraq before 2003. Today, six years on, their numbers have dwindled to 11,000 and they are mostly residing in Baghdad's predominantly Shi'i neighbourhood of Baladiyat. There are also roughly 2300 Palestinian refugees stranded awhile in different camps such as Al-Tanaf, Al-Ruweished, Al-Hol and Al-Waleed camps inside the neutral area or on the Iraqi-Syrian-Jordanian borders.

This visit to Irbil, not unlike the previous one undertaken to Baghdad, highlighted the mounting pressures that the Palestinian leadership faces in helping define the legal status and resettlement possibilities of those refugees. This becomes even more precarious in view of repeated assertions that Palestinians were awarded special privileges by Saddam Hussein so he could portray himself as the Arab leader par excellence championing the Palestinian cause and fighting against Western oppression. Although some Palestinians actually dispute the true extent of those privileges, there was clearly some sort of symbiotic relationship ratione personae, one of mutual benefit, that was not always equitable, and it is therefore fathomable if some Iraqis are upset with, or angry at, this ostensibly favoured treatment.

In this sense, therefore, my hope remains that the visits by Mahmoud Abbas to Baghdad and later Irbil will help tackle this chapter in the history of this refugee people. As a new volume is being written about the future of Iraq without a ruthless despot at its helm, it is perhaps time to help heal those open sores and expire those memories by charting the way for a better relationship between the two communities. It would not be inconceivable to argue that Abbas' abiding concern led him to Kurdistan in order to urge his hosts to exercise temporary welcome and hospitality to some of those refugees into Kurdistan. In one sense, by assisting the Palestinians in their present ordeal, the Kurds would help Iraq let its bygones be bygones. However, the understandable Kurdish fear is that a safe shelter for those refugees might well become a prelude to revising the prospects of settling Palestinians in northern Iraq.

The existential issue of statelessness

This existential issue of statelessness and the struggle of a people to belong to a land, highlight the second more symbolic issue emanating from the visit. It could be gleaned from Mr Barzani's welcome where he stated that "just as he [Mahmoud Abbas] is the first president to visit the region, we expect and we hope that the Palestinian consulate will be the first consulate to open in Irbil". Indeed, this open welcome echoes the fervent and decades-long wish of both Kurds and Palestinians for self-determination – a dream that has sustained the plural ethnic, religious, political and linguistic hopes of both peoples despite immense political, geo-strategic and global obstacles facing them.

But let me introduce a word of caution based on *realpolitik* as much as our own history and experience in Europe. As some SOMA readers are well aware, Europeans have paid a heavy price for their past jingoistic mistakes and many of us are now striving to move away from a narrow sense of ethno-nationalism toward more transparent cultures and open borders.

I can fully understand that millions of Kurds and Palestinians worldwide feel they are not at such a crossroads and would argue that they have not yet managed to secure fully their national rights. Whether this is true for some parties or questionable for others, the reality is that the map of the Middle East is being re-re-drawn differently today and both peoples must adapt their strategies to the new realities around them. Otherwise, the downside is that both peoples might end up anew paying too steep a price in a world that is far from being fair or just. Two peoples, two hopes, two futures: could those visits facilitate rapprochement between Palestinians and Kurds?

15 April 2009

Chapter 10

The deal of the century?

Prior to the narrow re-election of Benyamin Netanyahu as Prime Minister of Israel in April 2019 (explored further in Chapter 26 of this book), there has been endless speculation about a 'deal of the century' emerging in Israel–Palestine – speculations which vividly illustrate the gap between aspirations and realities in terms of finding a way forward.

In fact, one prediction crossing my radar suggested that the deal would perhaps provide $60 billion for the Palestinian Authority, $40 billion to Egypt as well as $20 billion to Jordan and Lebanon. It would highlight four principles – freedom, respect, security and opportunity – with one key goal of "developing infrastructure" for "tremendous growth in ... the West Bank and Gaza." It seems to me that the naïve – perhaps crude would be a more apposite adjective – reasoning presupposed that oodles of cash would ensure the acceptance of this deal. But it was equally clear to me that the deal would envisage shifting such a colossal financial burden to the US allies – which in blunt language meant some of the Gulf countries.

A recent Editorial by Sani Meo in an edition of *This Week in Palestine* magazine cast doubt that such a deal could ever be acceptable to a majority of ordinary Palestinians no matter the personalities, circumstances or consequences. I enjoyed Meo's piece because it was a sensible and local grassroots viewpoint that echoed the opinions of ordinary men and women who cannot easily be lured into a deal that promises them a lot of benefits, as well as many hardships, but also deprives them of their vision for a free Palestine. In fact, his piece underlined the fact that the US Administration refuses to understand that no Palestinian leader could acquiesce to a deal that essentially sells out Jerusalem. The last sentence in this editorial struck me when Meo also concluded:

> It is no secret that the deal of the century is meant to rid those regimes of the Palestinian 'nuisance', but as weak as those wretched Palestinians are, they hold the key to sabotaging a major political scheme that would change the strategic geopolitical situation of the area and possibly beyond. Without mincing words, the deal of the century is a no go.

So what about this plan that is purportedly meant to be unveiled after the Israeli parliamentary elections of 9 April and the formation of a new government in Israel? Let us go back a few months and examine some salient facts.

Facing political reality

Over many years, Palestinians have somehow acknowledged a few facts. A key fact is that Israel is uninterested in withdrawing from the occupied Palestinian territories. Rather, it is interested in the geography of these lands whilst attempting to rid itself of their demography. Otherwise put, keep the arable lands with their aquifers and get rid of those pesky Palestinian men, women and children who populate them and who challenge the monochromatic version of *Eretz Yisrael* (Land of Israel) and are a burden on the financial coffers of the State.

Palestinians have also acknowledged that the USA under all its presidents had an inbuilt political bias in favour of Israel and against Palestinians. Whether this is due to the standpoints of their legislative bodies in the Senate and Congress, to the impact of a community of Evangelical Christians or to lobbying organisations such as American Israel Public Affairs Committee (AIPAC), US presidents have tilted willy-nilly toward the Israeli Zionist version of a future peace pact whose genesis can be found in the shameful last chapter of the British Mandate. Whether US Presidents have been hard-nosed with the parties or paid lip service to Palestinian legitimate demands, the equation has been both uneven in the implementation of International law and unerringly skewed in its interpretation.

Furthermore, Palestinians have acknowledged that Europe is not really a weighty political player and clearly lacks a coherent common foreign policy. I remember Palestinian officials telling me that the USA makes the political decisions whist Europe provides the funding. Crudely put, America provided the military arsenal for Israel to bomb, damage or spoliate Palestinian territories and infrastructures, whereas Europe stepped in to repair or rebuild them.

Palestinians have moreover acknowledged – whether overtly or covertly – that many of the Arab countries are fed up to the teeth with the Palestinian conflict and want to find a way to get rid of this refugee-laden problem. Official statements or endorsements of the Palestinian rights have often been no more and no less than mere verbal placebos, and the dollars coming into the Palestinian coffers from some Arab states has been a way of 'throwing money at the problem'. But a key reason why they have demurred until recently from any more drastic action such as regular public meetings with Israeli officials, is the strong grassroots support that Palestinians enjoy across much of the Arab and Muslim countries. Rulers would prefer to pay token support to this cause, which, remember, was for decades the hub of all the conflicts in the Arab World rather than have to contend with the ire of their populace.

And finally, Palestinians have openly acknowledged that they are divided not only between the West Bank and Gaza but also amongst the different parties of those two territorial encampments. They remain in bitter disagreement over many issues. However, no matter the political algorithms of such disagreements, there are no more than a handful of Palestinians today (whether inside the Green Line or in the occupied Palestinian territories) who would accept forfeiture of the Palestinian right for self-determination and the establishment of an independent and sovereign state.

The Trump era and its implications

Much of what we have been talking about has changed with the emergence of President Donald Trump and his coterie of functionaries – including Jared Kushner, Jason D Greenblatt and David Friedman – who muddied the waters and encouraged rapacious attitudes. This president, transactional to his fingertips, but with a political *nous* that rivals a tailor's dummy, seems fixated by the monies of the Arab Gulf countries, and is paranoid (at least outwardly) over Iran. So he has been trying to shift the fulcrum from Palestine to Iran. Three Gulf Cooperation Council countries – Saudi Arabia, the UAE and Bahrain – have helped feed this paranoia as they seem more interested in countering Iranian hegemony than in securing a Palestinian independent state. The political environment that spawned the Saudi-tailored Arab Peace Initiative in Beirut (2002, reaffirmed in 2007 and 2017 simultaneously) is alas no more, and the façade of solidarity with Palestinians has been replaced with other egregious agendas that highlight elements of fear, control, impulsiveness and suppression.

In pursuing its focus on Iran, though, the current US Administration and its allies have tried to ride roughshod over Palestinian aspirations and lead them toward further concessions that are tantamount to an abject surrender of their rights and hopes for their own state. Lie on your backs and shut up, Palestinians have been told, and we will tickle your tummies with some morsels of territory and a bagful of money.

But when the Palestinians – divided, powerless, weary and challenged but resolute in their dignity – pushed back and refused to play ball, the US Administration decided to 'punish' Palestinians in the hope of coercing them to come back to the negotiating table in order to consider a "deal of the century" stewed in Jared Kushner's steamy kitchen. In other words, Palestinians were told that they had to forfeit their rights, put up with the new realities and move on.

Consequently, the US embassy was transported from Tel Aviv to Jerusalem, the Palestinian Mission in Washington DC was shuttered (and its representative assumed his new functions in London), the US Consulate-General in East Jerusalem was shut down, and all forms of financial monies were withheld from Palestinians. Israel was encouraged by the boldness of the US Administration to pursue its own brazen settler policies or tax-related financial restrictions, and some Arab League members hoped that the 'Palestinian problem' would be sorted out so they could focus on Iran. They whimpered and issued diplomatic exclamation marks that meant less than the decibels associated with them.

It's the land, stupid!

So what now? Has the Palestinian goose been well and truly cooked by these unilateral measures? To start with, I am not sure about the viability of the "ultimate deal". However, assuming that it will be midwifed at some stage, I was one of those people who had initially encouraged Palestinians not to turn it down outright but to play Israeli ministers at their own game with a 'yes, but' formula that is a classic in political negotiations. However, it seems to me that Palestinians will be put in such an unenviable position that their only option now is to reject a deal that ostensibly will try to win their approval by inducing them with financial hand-outs However, assuming that such financial largesse were even possible, I do not believe that an economic spurt would resolve what are two political narratives competing fiercely over land. Palestinians can be given enough money to create more start-up projects and financial investments, but their land will remain under occupation. I recall wryly the 'Advancing Conditions for Growth and Resilience' business-led push for Israeli-Palestinian peace, which took place on the shores of the Dead Sea in Jordan via the World Economic Forum in 2013. Despite the presentations by Yossi Vardi and Munib Al-Masri, the financial initiative failed starkly to break the political impasse.

In a phrase coined by his campaign strategist, President Bill Clinton said winningly during the 1992 presidential campaign, "It's the economy, stupid!". I would say today what I have reiterated for decades, "It's the land, stupid!" And if we fail to understand this irreversible causal nexus between 'land', 'occupation' and 'rights', we will quite soon find ourselves grappling with what is already morphing into an even bigger struggle for a binational state. So let me repeat for emphasis – "It's the land, stupid".

13 March 2019

Part Three: Reconciling Difference

Prologue

In order to look at how difference can be reconciled, on the basis of a just peace, it is necessary to understand the nature and grounds of that difference. That is the purpose of this section. We begin (chapter eleven, 2016) with a statement of the multivalent reality of the Israeli-Palestinian conflict, and an acute observation of the way in which what is at stake – freedom, dignity and statehood – can look rather different from multiple external locations, and from within the experience of those on the ground. Then in chapter twelve we shift gear to re-explore what that means in practical terms by examining the impulses towards a two-state or one-state solution through a reflection on the huge contribution of the late intellectual Edward Saïd (who died in 2003). The intersection of the aspirational and the political is further highlighted in chapter thirteen, which takes a detailed and critical look at United Nations Security Council Resolution 2334 (2016), with the land question very much to the fore. Next, in chapter fourteen, is a personal and profound reflection, with plenty of historical and sociological context, on the reality facing Christians in what is called the Holy Land (but sadly does not live up to that title) at present. Finally, the issue of reconciling the gap between resolution and reality at the political level is tackled in chapter fifteen, as the question of recognition of a Palestinian state is tackled. We end with a strong appeal to human and spiritual – including biblical – values and practices to re-ground the political task.

Chapter 11

Palestine: an ever-shrinking map without a road

In June 2016 I was invited to give a talk in Germany at the annual Synod of the European Diocese of the Church of England – with a brief to cover the Middle East, North Africa and the Gulf in just ninety minutes. Accepting the rather daunting challenge, I found myself focusing the beginning and end on my talk Palestine, the conflict that began in 1967 and which constitutes the longest and saddest story of occupation in modern history.

Why did I do that, given that the Arab Spring has been absent in the Palestinian territories and that the situation may have been seen to be relatively quiescent at the time? Some mischievous commentators are even opining that the conflict is being managed quite well: after all, Israel is not truly being sanctioned by the international community, and the Palestinians are not really starving, like many Syrians or Yemenis today.

Multiple differences in one

Quite true, but Palestine remains the granddaddy of all the conflicts in the Levant since before the British Mandate and the creation of the State of Israel. It embodies the biggest difference that has to be reconciled on the path to justice and peace. Forgive me if I keep reiterating that, but it is essential to grasp.

Buzz words like *nakba* and *naksa* or UNGAR 194 (on refugees) and UNSCR 224 or 338 (on the illegality of occupation) are part of the political lexicon of every Arab man or woman in the region. It is instinctive, nay intuitive, and therefore the Israel–Palestine conflict (with one predatory state and another virtual one) has been – and still abides as – a central feature of regional problems for Arabs and Muslims alike.

At its most reader-friendly level, the story of Palestine can be explored in Dr Ghada Al-Karmi's compelling book *In Search of Fatima*. However, Palestine is much more than a story that turned sour. It encapsulates elements of history, psychology and emotional investment. It highlights colonialism, betrayal and treachery.

It is even not solely about an epic struggle against the injustice and inequity perpetrated against the original inhabitants of this parcel of land by a Western world guilt-ridden about the Holocaust. Perhaps it is about a formula that turned into a master-and-slave equation between increasingly arrogant Israelis and pliantly subjugated Palestinians. What we are dealing here is not one difference and conflict, but multiple overlapping ones.

Having worked on the second-track negotiations of the Israeli-Palestinian conflict during the [now much-maligned] Oslo years, and having also advised the traditional Churches of Jerusalem about the political process, I am well aware that the solution to the conflict is within reach. If one looks at the various UN Resolutions, the Clinton Parameters, Taba in 2001, the Arab Peace Initiative of 2002 (re-endorsed in 2007), the Olmert-Abbas talks of 2008, as well as other moots, all of them support the critical inevitability of a two-state solution. Otherwise put, the only credible solution is the emergence of two states – Israel and Palestine – existing as neighbours next to each other.

But a cynic would wonder why Israel should cede territory it controls to the Palestinians? With a turgid ideology that matches its concrete separation wall, it can try to perpetuate the occupation. Yet, failure to reach agreement would either lead to the dangerous chaos and more apartheid-style control by Israel that breeds more violence, mayhem and – why not – ISIL-style radicalisation. Or else it would augur a binational one-state solution that coerces Israeli Jews and Palestinian Arabs (Muslims and Christians) living in one state, altering the demographics of this land in favour of Palestinian Arabs and inevitably turning into a tinderbox that spews out more vitriol and violence.

However, the present successive right-wing governments led by PM Benyamin Netanyahu have continued a policy of dispossessing Palestinians of their lands through a relentless plan of encroaching settlements and outposts that have been no more than illegal land-grabs which have been conducted with sheer impunity and a total disregard to International law, its Geneva Conventions and even EU foreign policy objectives. Just take a look at an MSNBC TV presentation of the four maps showing the gradual loss of Palestinian land from 1946 till the present day via the UN Plan of 1947 and the subsequent colonisation by Israel of Palestinian lands. It should become evident to the most colour-blind pundits or double-speak politicians that we are heading for disaster.

Yearning for justice

The solution consists not of constantly colliding two narratives, but rather of giving rise to two states alongside the Green Line with appropriate swaps or adjustments and creative diplomatic solutions to the core issues of Jerusalem, refugees, security and water. Otherwise, and whether we invoke Sisyphean or Promethean analogies to this festering conflict, the result will only spell disaster that will continue to haunt us despite the uprisings in the Middle East and North Africa (MENA) region.

And for those who refuse to wake up before it is too late, who are not too fretful about the human impact of the occupation on both victim and victimiser, or who are even lulled into a false sense of security or irredentist ideology, they should recall the experience of South Africa. Here was a country where one group had the power to rule over another and pen its native inhabitants into Bantustans. Yet, the inextinguishable human yearning for justice prevailed despite considerable odds until South Africa exited its nightmare. Ditto with Palestine too. The map is shrinking, the road may seem blocked, but there is still a way ahead in even the most apparently intractable of situations, as the end of apartheid showed.

19 June 2016

Chapter 12

Two states in one?

"Edward was a rare bird. He was both an icon and an iconoclast!" – Robert Fisk, *The Independent,* 26 September 2003

Professor Edward Saïd, a world-renowned scholar, writer and critic died last week. An outspoken advocate of Palestinian rights and a prominent Christian member of the Palestinian parliament-in-exile until 1991, he was also an arch critic of both Israeli practices and the Oslo Accords. Salman Rushdie once said that Saïd "reads the world as closely as he reads books". And the Irish critic Seamus Deane described him as "a truly public intellectual who has a powerful influence within the academy and also a potent public presence. He is a very brilliant reader, of both texts and political situations."

The last time I spoke at some length with Professor Saïd was at the American Colony hotel in Jerusalem. He looked old and frail – hunched over his breakfast cereals, a blanket covering his shoulders. He talked to me about his friendship and musical partnership with Daniel Barenboim and their joint attempts to straddle the Arab-Israeli divide through music. He also took me to task for defending a set of accords [Oslo] that he insisted fell short of granting Palestinians any legitimate and viable rights. I saw him one final time at a recent conference in London: the man had not mellowed, the ideas had not changed much, and the fiery zeal of a Palestinian in exile still irradiated his discourses. I shall miss the man – warts and all.

Edward Saïd had good reason to be a political sceptic. He sought reconciliation, but disagreed with its pathways to date. Indeed, a brief political somersault from Madrid to Oslo to the 'roadmap', and one draws the inevitable conclusion that Palestinians – and by osmosis Israelis – are getting a raw deal! Coming up with flawed 'peace processes' that are no more than mere guidelines with no fixed or finite destinations cannot convince either people to commit themselves to serious and painful compromises. The Quartet cannot overcome the mistrust, fear, trauma and polarisation on both sides of an ugly and piranha-like 'separation wall' without articulating end-goals or outcomes. Talking loosely about a settlement predicated upon International law, cessation of violence and two flags fluttering beside each other, is inadequate.

Which way forward?

It is true that many religious and secular organisations – international as much as Israeli or Palestinian – have been struggling relentlessly for years to achieve peace and reconciliation between the two peoples. However, and if one were to overlook the historical or legal matrices of this conflict, the fact remains that the overriding obstacle toward peace is the Israeli illegal occupation since 1967 of Palestinian land. That is what Edward Saïd stressed almost mantra-like to his interlocutors and audiences, and that is the major hub of this conflict. All the physical, psychological or structural forms of violence manifesting themselves in Israel and Palestine today find their roots in an unyielding and insidious occupation.

As the debilitating stalemate continues, Israelis and Palestinians continue their tussle. And they constantly find themselves alternating between the frying pan and the fire, checkmating each other or trying to seize the moral ground as a justification for further bloodletting, murders and crimes against fellow human beings. Simply reading Elizabeth Laird's new book, *A Little Peace of Ground,* gives a sour taste of the awful hardships Palestinian children face daily under occupation.

But without a Nelson Mandela, and without non-violent visions and strategies that meld both peoples together into the folds of a two-state solution, what is the alternative? If the two-state solution were indeed no longer physically possible due to the unbridled settlement policies pursued by Israel, and if demography is creating its own unalterable facts, what are we left with that can serve as a framework for a settlement?

Edward Saïd often advocated a one-state solution, insisting that the alternative premise for two states adjacent to each other was neither practicable nor realistic. Indeed, an ever-increasing number of people are now also questioning the hitherto stated belief that the Israeli-Palestinian conflict is ultimately resolvable via a territorial partition that would separate the Palestinians from the Israelis. Instead, the one-state option is once more taking the shape of a radical alternative that would seek a way out of the deadly cycle of violence. Such an option would advocate for equal political and civic rights in one state – one-man, one-vote.

By posting one homeland for both sides, the one-state solution not only does away with the conflict over history and legitimisation, but both sides can also maintain their 'right of return' without this being at the expense of the other, and Israeli settlers would not need to be removed from their settlements. Jerusalem could then also become the shared capital of a unitary Arab-Jewish state.

Clearly, irreconcilable differences appear at this stage. But despite the ideological narratives of Zionism on the one hand, and the Palestinian nationalist impulses on the other, is it not better to start considering again the paradigm of a one-state solution rather than slide inexorably towards segregation or drift even more dangerously towards escalating resistance and violence from both sides? After all, and unlike the two-state solution, the resilience of a democratic and secular unitary Arab-Jewish homeland is not contingent upon developments on the ground. It is a matter of a change of hearts and minds. And yes, as Professor Edward Saïd would have also reminded us, we do have the example of South Africa.

2 October 2003

Chapter 13

Israeli settlements, Palestinian lands

I wish to reflect on the significance (or perhaps, sadly, the lack of it) of United Nations Security Council Resolution 2334 (2016). Forgive me for commencing by quoting it in full, but this is important. It encapsulates a good deal in a relatively short space regarding Israeli settlements and Palestinian lands – the continuing crux of the conflict. The resolution reads as follows.

> The Security Council,
>
> Reaffirming its relevant resolutions, including resolutions 242(1967), 338 (1973), 446 (1979), 452 (1979), 465 (1980), 476 (1980), 478 (1980), 1397 (2002), 1515 (2003) and 185o (2008),
>
> Guided by the purposes and principles of the Charter of the United Nations, and reaffirming, inter alia, the inadmissibility of the acquisition of territory by force,
>
> Reaffirming the obligation of Israel, the occupying Power, to abide scrupulously by its legal obligations and responsibilities under the Fourth Geneva Convention relative to the Protection of Civilian Persons in Time of War, of 12 August 1949, and recalling the advisory opinion rendered on 9 July 2004 by the International Court of Justice,
>
> Condemning all measures aimed at altering the demographic composition, character and status of the Palestinian Territory occupied since 1967, including East Jerusalem, including, inter alia, the construction and expansion of settlements, transfer of Israeli settlers, confiscation of land, demolition of homes and displacement of Palestinian civilians, in violation of international humanitarian law and relevant resolutions,
>
> Expressing grave concern that continuing Israeli settlement activities are dangerously imperilling the viability of the Two-State solution based on the 1967 lines,
>
> Recalling the obligation under the Quartet Roadmap, endorsed by its resolution 1515 (2003), for a freeze by Israel of all settlement activity, including "natural growth", and the dismantlement of all settlement outposts erected since March 2001,
>
> Recalling also the obligation under the Quartet roadmap for the Palestinian Authority Security Forces to maintain effective operations aimed at confronting all those engaged in terror and dismantling terrorist capabilities, including the confiscation of illegal weapons,
>
> Condemning all acts of violence against civilians, including acts of terror, as well as all acts of provocation, incitement and destruction,
>
> Reiterating its vision of a region where two democratic States, Israel and

Palestine, live side by side in peace within secure and recognized borders,

Stressing that the *status quo* is not sustainable and that significant steps, consistent with the transition contemplated by prior agreements, are urgently needed in order to (i) stabilize the situation and to reverse negative trends on the ground, which are steadily eroding the two-State solution and entrenching a one-State reality, and (ii) to create the conditions for successful final status negotiations and for advancing the two-State solution through those negotiations and on the ground,

1. Reaffirms that the establishment by Israel of settlements in the Palestinian territory occupied since 1967, including East Jerusalem, has no legal validity and constitutes a flagrant violation under international law and a major obstacle to the achievement of the two-State solution and a just, lasting and comprehensive peace;

2. Reiterates its demand that Israel immediately and completely cease all settlement activities in the occupied Palestinian territory, including East Jerusalem, and that it fully respects all of its legal obligations in this regard;

3. Underlines that it will not recognize any changes to the 4 June 1967 lines, including with regard to Jerusalem, other than those agreed by the parties through negotiations;

4. Stresses that the cessation of all Israeli settlement activities is essential for salvaging the Two-State solution, and calls for affirmative steps to be taken immediately to reverse the negative trends on the ground that are imperilling the Two-State solution;

5. Calls upon all States, bearing in mind paragraph 1 of this resolution, to distinguish, in their relevant dealings, between the territory of the State of Israel and the territories occupied since 1967;

6. Calls for immediate steps to prevent all acts of violence against civilians, including acts of terror, as well as all acts of provocation and destruction, calls for accountability in this regard, and calls for compliance with obligations under international law for the strengthening of ongoing efforts to combat terrorism, including through existing security coordination, and to clearly condemn all acts of terrorism;

7. Calls upon both parties to act on the basis of international law, including international humanitarian law, and their previous agreements and obligations, to observe calm and restraint, and to refrain from provocative actions, incitement and inflammatory rhetoric, with the aim, inter alia, of de-escalating the situation on the ground, rebuilding trust and confidence, demonstrating through policies and actions a genuine commitment to the two-State solution, and creating the conditions necessary for promoting peace;

8. Calls upon all parties to continue, in the interest of the promotion of peace and security, to exert collective efforts to launch credible negotiations on all final status issues in the Middle East peace process and within the time frame specified by the Quartet in its statement of 21 September 2010;

9. Urges in this regard the intensification and acceleration of international and regional diplomatic efforts and support aimed at achieving, without delay a comprehensive, just and lasting peace in the Middle East on the basis of the rel-

evant United Nations resolutions, the Madrid terms of reference, including the principle of land for peace, the Arab Peace Initiative and the Quartet Roadmap and an end to the Israeli occupation that began in 1967; and underscores in this regard the importance of the ongoing efforts to advance the Arab Peace Initiative, the initiative of France for the convening of an international peace conference, the recent efforts of the Quartet, as well as the efforts of Egypt and the Russian Federation;

10. Confirms its determination to support the parties throughout the negotiations and in the implementation of an agreement;

11. Reaffirms its determination to examine practical ways and means to secure the full implementation of its relevant resolutions;

12. Requests the Secretary-General to report to the Council every three months on the implementation of the provisions of the present resolution;

13. Decides to remain seized of the matter.

An analysis – words lacking implementation

After much deliberation at the United Nations, and also between governments, and following a critical few moments when some observers thought that the Security Council would blink away from addressing this thorny issue, Resolution 2334 was adopted on 23 December 2016 with 14 votes in favour and one abstention. And the 14 votes (four permanent and nine non-permanent members) that supported the much-edited Resolution became less important – although Israel censured them via their ambassadors in Tel Aviv – because the focus was on the United States, which broke its longstanding tradition and did not use its veto to firewall Israel from this Resolution.

Having toiled for well over two decades on the Israeli-Palestinian conflict, can I claim to be enthused by this moment of history? Did this latest UNSCR define in some way the future of the Israeli-Palestinian conflict?

My simple answer is 'no' – and certainly not for the short or even medium terms. So here are my four core observations about this Resolution, one that has been hailed and maligned in equal measure by the different parties:

It has certainly not escaped anybody's notice that New Zealand and Senegal were the main non-permanent members of the Security Council to 'push' this Resolution. For me, this is key, because Egypt was the initial sponsor. However, it succumbed to external pressures and withdrew the draft. This is another example of how Egypt has alas been dwarfed politically. It was once the leader of the whole Arab World. In fact, both Anwar Sadat and Hosni Mubarak had somehow managed to maintain a fig leaf of support for the Palestinian cause.

Now, Egypt is fast becoming an apostrophe in international politics. Not only is such Egyptian irrelevance deleterious to the interests of the region, it will impact intra-Arab relations too. More so since many of the GCC have constantly striven to support Egypt with lavish financial aid. Mind you, what is equally galling is that whilst Israel was excoriating the countries that voted in favour of the Resolution, hardly any Arab country thought it appropriate to express their support for New Zealand and Senegal or for the other eleven countries.

The press has highlighted that Israeli Prime Minister was furious with this Resolution. I would go a step further and add that he carefully stage-managed his hysteria with cynicism. After all, although the illegality of settlements was last discussed thirty-eight long years ago in 1979, it has nonetheless remained a constant policy of all US [Republican and Democratic] Administrations. So the arrogance of Benyamin Netanyahu in expecting – demanding – the same insulation time and again while creating new peace-unfriendly facts on the ground is simply staggering.

But this arrogant expectation is compounded further by an even bigger arrogance that he, and his right-wing allies, perpetuate about the Occupied Palestinian Territories. The way in which they colonise the lands that do not belong to them and then build outposts or settlements on them is not only self-righteous but also unlawful. It is like a thief stealing one's home, and then bullying the rightful owner of the house that s/he has no right to reclaim the house ... because it belongs to the thief after all. This is a form of political banditry.

However, my lack of enthusiasm has little to do with Arab inertia or Israeli histrionics. It has much more to do with the fact that this Resolution will not make a whisper of a difference to ordinary Palestinians who are being gradually dispossessed of their lands while their cause is being mothballed by many Arab and world leaders. The UN is replete with Resolutions – both at the Security Council and General Assembly – condemning Israeli occupation of Palestinian land. And yet none made a difference over the past 50+ years (my starting point remains June 1967) or helped create a two-state solution.

The formula of land-for-peace, so much mooted and pilloried in UNSCR 242 and subsequent Resolutions, let alone at the potholed Oslo process, remains unenforced – and perhaps also unenforceable. In my opinion, this latest Resolution will not either, since it has no implementation mechanisms in its 13 clauses. Besides, Israel has said it will ignore it. Except perhaps that it is yet another chapter in the

International law arsenal that could be invoked in some far and unpredictable future.

The core of the tragedy though is that the Palestinian territories that are being peopled with illegal settlers is gradually making the two-state solution harder to implement on the ground. Today, there are well over 430,000 Israeli settlers living in the West Bank. Another 200,000 Israelis live in east (largely Arab) Jerusalem too. So given the land-grab policies of successive Israeli governments, both Labour and Likud, and the blackmailing power of some coalition members within the Israeli cabinet, we could end up with the option of a unitary/one-state solution that pre-supposes equal rights for Israelis and Palestinians.

I cannot imagine this being acceptable to the majority of Israelis, nor to an overwhelmed Palestinian Authority for that matter. Conversely, Israel will have to rule over – and subsidise – three million Palestinians under the obligations defined by the Geneva Conventions, and this will become a recipe not only for economic and social disaster but also for inevitable apartheid-like practices.

I find it an example of post-truth populism (yes, both those quaint expressions go together quite well in this context) when some Israelis – not least politicians the likes of Yuval Steinitz or Miri Regev – start questioning whether the USA is indeed a friend of Israel when it provides the Jewish State with $38 billion of aid spread over 10 years.

Moreover, I am a tad uncertain of the hurried social media claims that President Obama instructed Samantha Power to abstain simply to spite Prime Minister Benyamin Netanyahu. Rather, I would argue that he calculated aloofly that President-Elect Donald J Trump would destroy any residual hope for a two-state solution anyway and so decided to salvage his own legacy with this last-minute manoeuvre.

Grounds for pessoptimism

So am I enthused by UNSCR 2334 (2016)? Sadly not, as I truly believe that the time will come soon when Mr Netanyahu will have to come clean and choose between settlements and the two-state solution. It is pointless for him to express outrage and suggest that this Resolution was the last straw that broke the camel's back. Even unfettered chutzpah has its checkpoints! Surely he cannot have his cake and eat it forever. Or can he?

Occupation of land and the two-state option are antithetical. However, being a lifelong pessoptimist, I would hope to be proven wrong if only for the sake of my Palestinian and Israeli friends' futures. So perhaps the redeeming grace of this UN drama is that it will make those choices starker for all those sitting on the fence. However, the proof of the pudding remains in the eating, and I do not see anyone eating the pudding ... yet.

27 December 2016

Chapter 14

We are Christians of the Holy Land

Haig is an Armenian Christian from Jerusalem, a city that is six miles and 20 minutes north of Bethlehem. Haig also happens to be my younger brother, and our family have lived in Jerusalem ever since 1915 when my grandparents fled Ottoman Turkey to Palestine during the Armenian genocide. Indeed, Bethlehem and Jerusalem, the fulcra of the Nativity and Resurrection of our Christian faith, were once bustling with local Christians. In Jerusalem, two of the four quarters of the Old City (the Christian and Armenian ones) are a living testimony to their centuries-old presence. Yet, today, although my brother and his family have steadfastly chosen to remain in Jerusalem, scores of Christians have left in search of more dignified, politically stable and economically viable alternatives.

So what do Christians witness in this land of frequent pilgrimages but also of infrequent visions?

Change and decline

Some sixty short years ago, Christians constituted roughly 25 per cent of the overall Palestinian population in the Holy Land, and around 80 per cent of Bethlehem, Beit Sahour and Beit Jala. Today, those numbers have dwindled drastically – in Bethlehem, for instance, they are just over 15 per cent of the overall population – largely because of the conflict between Israel and the Palestinians. No matter how people choose to interpret facts or massage realities, the political situation has been – and remains – the primary cause for the alarming reduction in the number of indigenous Christians in this biblical land. Christians have almost lost hope in a land that witnessed the incarnation of our hope. Dr Bernard Sabella, a sociologist who is also Executive Secretary of the Department on Service to Palestinian Refugees and Member of the Palestinian Legislative Council, has published numerous statistical studies on the haemorrhaging outflow of local Christians. In one study as far back as 2004, he estimated that local Christians now stood at far less than 2 per cent of the overall population, suggesting that this decline reflected a dearth in socio-economic and political visions for Palestine.

Over the past forty-three years, since the Israeli occupation of

Palestinian land in June 1967, Israeli rapacious settlers have colonised Palestinian land – often aided, and frequently abetted, by successive Israeli governments. The physical, demographic and economic integrity of the land – and thereby of the people living on it – has been eroded by deliberate Israeli policies that are not only contrary to International law and UN Resolutions but that also strive to get rid of Palestinian demography (the people) whilst retaining Palestinian geography (the land). In Bethlehem as in many other parts of the West Bank, an ugly separation wall encircles relentlessly the Palestinian areas, dividing one Palestinian from another, one institution from another. With secondary and smaller cement walls buttressing this wall, and with Israeli Jews-only settlements on Palestinian land, along with four-hundred checkpoints severing towns and villages from each other, Palestinian resources are being snuffed out and have resulted in the creation of small gaols within those territories. The concomitant consequences have been unemployment, poverty, socio-economic meltdown, despair and violence. Is it still any wonder that Palestinian Christians are leaving in droves?

In a speech on 29 April 2010, Professor John J. Mearsheimer, the R. Wendell Harrison Distinguished Service Professor of Political Science and co-director of the Program on International Security Policy at the University of Chicago, described some Israelis as the New Afrikaners. Indeed, such corrosive apartheid (separateness in Afrikaans) policies are being exercised by Israel in many Palestinian territories (where Christians live in small numbers amongst Palestinian Muslims). Is it also any wonder that some prominent Christian church and lay leaders issued the *Kairos Palestine Document: A Moment of Truth* in December 2009 in which they spoke out in liberation theology native terms about faith, hope and love in the heart of Palestinian suffering and against those practices that have condemned their communities to this downward spiral? Can such weakened communities resist any longer?

Christian–Muslim relations and Western Christianity

However, in focusing upon the sinister effects of Israeli occupation, it is equally scrupulous to look at other concerns befalling Palestinian Christians in this once-golden land (as the prophet Zechariah described it). Two contributory strains, I would opine, are Christian–Muslim relations and Western Christianity. When I was Ecumenical Consultant for the Churches of Jerusalem during the unlucky Oslo years, I recall how church leaders or their representatives would help nip in the bud any potential strife between Christians and Muslims by calling the late Chairman Yasser Arafat's representatives to seek their prompt mediation.

Today, those conduits of conflict resolution are far more complex and much less discernible, and the tensions between Palestinian Christians and Muslims are perceptibly more frequent even if most Palestinians would deny them vehemently due to an overall – anxious – sense of nationalism. I believe this is due in part to a growing political Islamisation within specific cross-sections of Palestinian society in the West Bank (and certainly in Gaza, with its tiny pocket of Christians and their public institutions) today.

Some Muslims have become less inclusive, spurn diversity and openly or secretly consider non-Muslims as infidels who do not belong to the land. Such attitudes are due to an ill-considered, even blinkered, belief that the links those Christians have with the larger Universal Church in the West (Greece, Rome or London) could turn them into politically potential fifth columns. I have heard Palestinians speaking out – often discreetly – about some practices of physical and structural violence whereby Christian shops are the last ones to be frequented for business and where Palestinian Christians are the last to receive financial aid from local authorities. Engage a Christian deacon, ironmonger, butcher, secretary, verger, or physician, and one detects those worries simmering under the chipped veneer of pan-Palestinian solidarity.

This is an unfortunate development that is neither Islamic nor provides proper *ijtihad,* or jurisprudence. But it is occasionally detracting from the collective effort necessary to focus on the central objective of Israeli occupation and is alas a reality that increasingly blights the lives of everyday Christians.

But is the radicalisation of some pockets of Islam the sole reason why a small but important number of Palestinian Muslims are looking charily at Palestinian Christians? Has Palestine become an almost Lebanese clone where confessional politics are taking hold of what has for long decades been a fiercely secular and inclusive society? I for one remember growing up in a neighbourhood of northern Jerusalem that had many Muslims who were not only 'neighbours' but also friends. I am sure that Haig could tell stories about his own experiences of friendships and respectful coexistence. After all, Palestinians had almost always been united by their political aims, not divided by their religious affiliations. One cannot also forget that some of the incipient Palestinian liberation leaders were Christian, as are politicians, parliamentarians and ambassadors today. It is not always helpful to turn into an ostrich in the midst of a sand dune either.

Christian fundamentalism

I suggest that the tensions fomented by Islamist radicalism, over and above the Israeli rampant occupation of land, are also exacerbated by fundamentalist evangelical Christian constituencies in the West (largely in the USA) who purport that the Christian faith equates itself with an unquestioning support for Israel. They claim this is because God chose the Israelites as His people and entered into a Covenant with them. It is therefore the duty of Christians, those groups claim, to defend Israel (a political entity) and Israelis (a demographic entity) over the whole of biblical land of Israel (a geographic entity).

In my view, such Christians are not only limited in their faith-based periscope but are also ostracising 'other' Christians by adhering rigidly to the tenets of the Old Testament, ignoring the transformative message of the New Testament, being selective in their scriptural and prophetic quotations, and releasing Israelis from their obligations in relation to their covenant with God let alone toward Palestinians. Surely, to be hemmed in by a faith perception that is literalist or exclusivist is not how our Lord and Saviour will have acted today. But such Christians also believe the only way for the Messiah to return to earth (and therefore fulfil prophesies in the Book of Revelation) is through the in-gathering of Jews (in modern-day Israel) so they could be converted to Christianity and pave the way for the Second Coming of Christ.

I cannot frankly see many Jews getting terribly excited by this Christian plan! But there exists today a finite tactical alliance whereby Jews overlook the underlying eschatological motivations of some Western Christians in return for their unstinting financial and political support of Israel. The Old Testament has become the organic nexus between [some] Christians and [some] Jews, at the expense of the New Testament and the indigenous followers of Christ region-wide.

Pilgrims of faith and conviction

So where do we Christians of the Holy Land stand today as pilgrims of faith on our journeys of faith? I believe that the three existential challenges I highlighted are together leading some Palestinian Christians to re-calculate constantly their options. HB Michel Sabbah, emeritus patriarch of Jerusalem, delivered a lecture entitled The Theological, Spiritual and Pastoral Christian Presence in the Middle East at CEDRAC in Beirut on 5th May in which he affirmed that Palestinian Christians are cross-bearing witnesses, whose commandment is one of love, of showing how to build a healthy and inclusive society, and of being true bridges with the outside world. I suppose one could add that Jews, Christians and Muslims are united through Abraham and Sarah, hewn from the same rock (Is 51:1), and so it becomes quintessential to find ways for co-existence in this land between the three monotheistic faiths.

But how does one affirm the Christian presence in the Holy Land? In Bethlehem, for instance, in order to dissuade young Palestinian families from leaving the Holy Land, the Franciscan Order is building new flats and offering them to young Palestinian couples in return for low-rent tenancies. This is a practical – and critical – tool to help counter emigration. But if we mean to tackle the root causes of the problems facing Christians in the Holy Land today rather than paper over the symptoms alone, the first station should be an end to Israeli occupation and its illegal practices. Palestinians must be set free from captivity, imprisonment, separation walls, settlements, ID confiscations and allowed instead to pursue their own destinies and hopes – and to make their own mistakes. Only then could they be expected to put their own house in order – presently in shambles – and become accountable as they edify at long last their independent state.

To those friends world-wide worried about the Christian life, presence and witness across the whole Middle East, I remind them of St Cyril of Jerusalem (315-386) – a contemporary of Epiphanius, Jerome and Rufinus – who stated, "Do not rejoice in the cross in time of peace only, but hold fast to the same faith in time of persecution also. Do not be a friend of Jesus in time of peace only but also in time of persecution." Perhaps we should all learn – I before you – to be less à la carte Christians with anaemic faiths and to show instead resoluteness, fortitude and solidarity in our outreach to our neighbours during times of adversity.

Cautious hope
This is why I am also cautiously hopeful that the forthcoming Special Assembly of the Synod of Bishops for the Middle East called for by HH Pope Benedict XVI that will take place in Rome from 10-24 October 2010 will manage to discuss carefully, but also openly and judiciously,

those three existential issues. The theme of the Synod is The Catholic Church in the Middle East: Communion and Witness and is underscored by the scriptural verse 'Now the company of those who believed were of one heart and soul' (Acts 4. 32). In this respect, the Catholic Bishops' Conference of England and Wales in London, supported by its counterparts in Germany and the USA, will provide support and exposure to this event that will unite all the Catholic Church leadership of the Middle East under one roof in the Vatican.

So today, I invite my readers to spare no effort in reaching out with love, prayer but also action to those quarantined 'Living Stones' (1 Peter 2. 5) who face the daily vagaries of life in the presence of human pain and unholy conflicts. Our Christocentric faith does not call for apathy, nor should it pander to hyper-inflated political correctness or jaundiced cynicism. What it exacts from us can perhaps be summed up for me by St Paul's Letter to the Ephesians to seek the unity of the spirit in the bond of peace (Ephesians 4. 3). Can we all "do our small bit" and pursue our mission and help ensure that those Living Stones do not inevitably become the deadened sites of the Holy Land and of the wider Middle East?

3 July 2010

Chapter 15

Palestine between virtual and real independence

On 13 October 2014 the House of Commons debated a motion that was scheduled by the Backbench Business Committee following representations from Grahame M. Morris MP, Crispin Blunt MP, Sir Bob Russell MP, Caroline Lucas MP and Jeremy Corbyn MP. The Motion simply stated:

> That this House believes that the Government should recognise the state of Palestine alongside the state of Israel, as a contribution to securing a negotiated two state solution.

After a lengthy debate, MPs voted 274 to 12 on division (Division 54) to approve the motion recognising Palestine.

Then on 22 October, the Seanad Éireann, Ireland's Senate or Upper House of Parliament, also passed a motion similar to the British one calling on the government in Dublin to recognise a Palestinian state. It received cross-party support and so did not require a vote. And much as it was also a symbolic vote that cannot change government policy, Ireland nonetheless became the third country to support recognition of 'Palestine' and undergirded the latest boost for those campaigning in favour of international recognition. Senator Averil Power from the center-right Fianna Fáil (Republican Party), speaking in the Dublin Senate debate accused Israel of having erected an 'apartheid regime'.

The Irish motion, quite similar to the British one and not far from the statements by the Swedish Foreign Minister earlier, called on the "government to formally recognise the state of Palestine and do everything it can to help secure a viable two-state solution to the Israeli-Palestinian conflict so that citizens of both states can live in peace and security."

The gulf between resolutions and realities

Yet despite those legislative and non-binding political moves – and it seems there are other similar moves afoot in Spain and France – such independence is still nothing more than a pipedream. Granted, the international community has a key role to play as facilitator or even initiator and mediator, but the gritty – and painfully responsible – decisions can only be taken by Israel. To recognise or not to recognise a Palestinian independence is a jaw-clenching challenge for Israel today.

So let me comment on one issue that often gnaws at my conscience. Almost every historian, lawyer or politician from different parties in Israel knows full well that East Jerusalem, the West Bank and Gaza are defined under International law and the Fourth Geneva Convention as territories occupied by Israel in 1967. Yet, despite the fact that many Israeli forward-looking organisations, authors, pundits and even politicians know that this landmass is under occupation and should go to Palestinians, successive Israeli governments have resolutely used every textbook on denial, procrastination and prevarication to avoid releasing most lands to their rightful owners.

Moreover, Israel has altered both the geography and demography of those lands by building illegal settlements and outposts across Jerusalem and the West Bank and colonising Palestinian space with subsidised Jewish residents. So much so that historical Palestine has almost shrunk to a few blotches drenched with massive Israeli conglomerations.

Therefore, my key question today is not strictly political in terms of either the merits or demerits of the case for Palestinian independence. That is after all quite easy: according to a raft of legal and political decisions, Israel should return the swathe of occupied territories back to Palestinians on the basis of the inclusive Arab Initiative of 2002 and a host of well-established parameters so both peoples can move forward and help create – in the words of none other than Shimon Peres – a Middle East of biblical milk and honey.

In other words, Israelis should desist from hiding behind biblical exegeses written many millennia ago or else project arguments that are anachronistic at best to delay the inevitable. But alas, Israel as a pioneering people has turned exceedingly arrogant, greedy and unjust toward others.

Humanity and faith beyond politics

So minus any political prognostication, what is my blunt – call it wholesomely naïve – apolitical question right now? Simply put, it is this: how do many Israeli politicians divest themselves of their very humanity, their sense of truth and justice in order to trample over other peoples' rights or go into paroxysms of anger and self-righteousness every time they are challenged about the occupation of another people? Why is it so hard for them to be true to the welfare of their peoples by admitting an irredentist truth, acting upon it and then helping build a less bellicose and a less unfair world?

Frankly, I often do not know what lurks in the minds of those decision-makers and purveyors of obfuscation. Yet, I do know how they affect me personally. As someone who was involved in second-track negotiations on behalf of the Churches of Jerusalem during the Oslo process, I went to Kikar Rabin (Rabin Square) in Tel Aviv once and spoke about the murdered Yitzhak Rabin as an erstwhile foe who might not have become a *chaver* (friend) for Palestinians if he had lived long enough but rather a deft architect of peace. I admire Israeli achievements over six decades – not least in hi-tech – but the scornful suppression of justice for Palestinians intuitively provokes in me human counter-reactions.

Is political candour not *de rigueur* anymore? Are truth and justice obsolescent? In fact, would the world get so much worse if Israel were to return the occupied territories? "I am for peace; but when I speak, they are for war" (Psalm 120. 7). Yet we often sadly but wilfully camouflage our guilt with naked untruths or, at best, with stark half-truths.

27 October 2014

Part Four: Bringing Change

Prologue

In order to be able truly to bear the weight of change, we first have to negotiate the burden of reality. These are the issues that come into sharp focus in this section of the book. Chapter sixteen begins by charting the 'one step forward, two steps back' feeling that has bedeviled progress on Israel–Palestine for years, examining the forces of inertia and setting out how change needs to be embraced. In chapter seventeen these tough issues of enduring political intransigence in the region are framed by reflections from the perhaps unlikely pairing of theologian Dr Rowan Williams and atheist philosopher Jean-Paul Satre – reminding us forcefully that the change process is also about the hearts and minds of those who bear our hope for the future. The next two chapters examine the extent to which international diplomacy (in these examples, President Obama in 2013 and Pope Francis in 2014) does and does not contribute towards unblocking political processes. Finally, we have an article from 2012, written eighteen months to two years after the genesis of the Arab Spring, looking at the impact of a much more resonant and powerful 'voice of the people', partly enabled by the exponential growth of digital mobilisation and news sharing. This is also a reminder that it is people themselves who need to be agents of their own destiny, not unaccountable and autocratic regimes.

Chapter 16

One step forward, two steps back

"You'll never silence the voice of the voiceless!" – Abahlali baseMjondolo shack-dwellers' movement in South Africa

I bring some unsettling news: the Palestinian cause, and with it the future destiny of Jerusalem, are gradually waning from the volatile Arab psyche and are in the process losing the centrality they have held in the Arab – and broadly Muslim – political imagination since 1948.

Only last week [September 2009], when Palestinians were protesting against settlements as well as intrusions on the esplanade of Al Haram al-Sharif, Egyptians and Algerians – and with them many others in the Arab World – were far more obsessed by a football game at Umm Durman in Sudan. Indeed, the destiny of the football match had galvanised the pride of Egyptians and Algerians in a way that Palestine and the fate of Jerusalem seemingly fail to do anymore.

I am being neither insulting nor flippant in saying this. The qualification of the Algerian team for the World Cup (1-0) was an important morale booster for many Arabs who are dispossessed of any real present-day achievement in our global world. In fact, this result restored the pride of one country (Algeria) even as it destroyed that of another (Egypt) and provoked many violent incidents and tit-for-tat punitive actions.

But in reality the attention of the large masses has shifted away from the Palestinian conflict that had inhabited Middle Eastern politics for decades. While ordinary Palestinians in the occupied territories are suffering increasingly more the impunity of an unjust occupation with all its attendant physical, economic and moral consequences, much of the Arab leadership – starting, dare I add, with the Palestinian leaderships both in the West Bank and Gaza – seems to have placed the destiny of this disempowered people on a back-burner. What we see is classic Arab inertia at a time when the settlement drive continues unabated under Benyamin Netanyahu's government despite its illegality under International law.

Retrogression analysed

Only this week, we learned that 900 new flats are to be built in the Gilo settlement in East Jerusalem, and that there also are fears concerning the excavations taking place in the periphery of the Haram al-Sharif / Temple Mount which could reportedly undermine the foundations of the Dome of the Rock and Al-Aqsa mosques. But Arab and Muslim attention seems distracted, and the slogans of solidarity and brotherhood from Arab leaders go hand-in-hand with apathy and inaction. Imagine the twist of irony: planeloads get sent to Sudan to cheer the national football players, and then other planeloads evacuate supporters back to the safety of their own country, whilst the Rafah border crossing between Egypt and southern Gaza remains shut in the face of life-seeking Palestinians.

In this staggering mess that is the bread and butter of many pundits with their op-eds, I would not actually mind being Benyamin Netanyahu – or even his hard-nosed foreign minister Avigdor Lieberman, since his defence minister does not register much on my political blip-meter these days – for he not only has his cake but he can eat it too. Not only are most Arabs divided and unfocused, let alone politically pusillanimous and strategically insignificant, Israel has equally succeeded to stare down the Obama Administration with its steadfast refusal to give in to the American demands for a full freeze on settlements.

There is such political dyslexia in much of the Arab World that Turkey – an erstwhile arch-foe of Arabs due to bitter memories spanning four centuries of colonisation – has now become the defender of Palestinian rights. Its foreign minister Ahmet Davutoglu, the Henry Kissinger of Turkey, postulated in his latest book *Strategic Depth – The International Position of Turkey,* the famous neighbourhood policy of 'zero problem' by playing quite deftly the dual political game of keeping one foot in the Western / American camp and the other in the Arab and Muslim worlds. Truly remarkable: you need a mediator for Iran? Turkey is there. You seek a resumption of Syrian-Israeli negotiations? Turkey is ready again. You would like to witness reconciliation between the West Bank and Gaza political leaderships? Turkey is ready too. But Turkey is also there in Iraq, in Kurdistan recently, and yet also maintains steadfastly its strategic alliance with Israel.

So I say hurray to Israel and also to Turkey, but cast a critical look at Palestinians and at the Arab World. As for the US and EU, the former is weighed down with a myriad other domestic and international agendas and can ill-afford any high-noon confrontation with Israel, whilst the latter that still bankrolls some Palestinian projects is a disparate collection of politicians with watered-down structures (just consider the real (in)significance of the recent EU elections of a new president and foreign minister) that carries little political weight and plays a pale role within a defunct roadmap process headed by an inglorious envoy [Tony Blair] whose vision has become that of an inflated but expired politician in an oversized corporation.

From despair to re-embracing change?

But why are we in such dire straits, and why is there a feeling of failure? Has the global economic recession redrawn all the priorities? Have Afghanistan and Iraq totally stolen the political attention of the world away from Palestine? Valid and expedient reasons, but the fact is that much of the Arab World has surrendered its genuine interest in the Palestinian national rights, and this has been exacerbated by inept Palestinian leaders compounding a lamentable stalemate with a range of wrong choices. If you cannot defend your own case, why should you expect your neighbours to be more proactive than yourself? And why should you wait for Israel to be cooperative if it can achieve its political designs and get away with them?

Many major *faux pas* have together catalysed this abortive situation. It began with the political spat between Fatah in the West Bank and Hamas in Gaza when the latter mounted a putsch against Mahmoud Abbas' leadership and wrested control of Gaza in 2007. This was hugely wrong in its own right, as it set the overall decline of the Palestinian cause in motion, and was unfortunately aided and abetted by Palestinian politicians in Gaza who were meant to ensure that such a catastrophe did not occur but who fled the Strip instead. However, having said that, every single month since that fateful divorce between those two important factions has entrenched further the divisions between different ideologies. There is an Islamist agenda in Gaza, a more secular one in the West Bank, a West that stoked the fires by supporting one party totally at the expense of the other, and an Israeli war against Gaza that is an indirect manifestation of its broader war against Palestinian nationalism. All have come together to produce a set of irreconcilable dynamics that have rendered the Palestinian cause less relevant today.

But the decline does not stop with the internecine feuds and the Israeli war on Gaza. What really withered the Palestinian diplomatic stamina is its official stance to the Goldstone Report of 15th September. This powerful report was authored by a former South African judge, former prosecutor for the war crimes' trials for former Yugoslavia and

Rwanda, and one of the most respected international jurists world-wide.

Officially titled *Human Rights in Palestine and Other Occupied Arab Territories: Report of the United Nations Fact Finding Mission on the Gaza Conflict,* it used voluminous amounts of information from multiple sources to hold Israel and Hamas accountable to the same standards of law and morality, making it clear that both sides must be assessed and held responsible mutatis mutandis for their actions. It suggested doing so by a series of actions by both sides to credibly investigate their conduct in the conflict. If no such probes took place, it called upon the international community to act through the UN Security Council or the International Criminal Court (ICC).

This report was a political gift for PA President Mahmoud Abbas and his team. Yet, instead of attempting to support a resolution by the United Nations Human Rights Council on allegations that Israel had committed war crimes in its attack on Gaza last year, the Palestinian leadership buckled under intense Israeli and American pressure and deferred consideration of this report. Just imagine what happened here: Palestinians shot themselves in the foot by opting out of a rare opportunity to indict Israeli actions in Gaza as well as Hamas reactions from within Gaza itself. Instead, they manifested a negligent indifference – political, ethical and juridical – that is truly mind-boggling. Coming on the heels of the report by Richard Falk, UN Rapporteur, that Israel had deliberately obstructed the work of humanitarian personnel by leaving the poor without basic medical, food and other services in violation of both international humanitarian law and human rights law, the 575-page Goldstone Report had documented serious violations of international humanitarian law by Israel, with some incidents amounting to war crimes and possible crimes against humanity, including wilful killings, deliberate attacks on civilian objects, wanton destruction of civilian property, indiscriminate attacks, the use of human shields, and collective punishment against Gazan civilian population in the form of a continuing blockade.

External pressure

However, the Palestinian leadership relented to US pressure not to act on the report with a flimsy pretext that it needed to build up its case and have it re-considered more forcefully in March 2010. In so doing, its credibility was left in tatters and the Palestinian cause suffered another setback. The political irony is that the Palestinians should have forged ahead with a consideration of the report by the UNHRC since the US will have vetoed it down anyway. After all, the Obama Administration rejected the report only days after its release, and the US House of Representatives had also moved to pass a non-binding resolution criticising and rejecting it. But instead of exposing old US double-standards even under a new US Administration, or even exercising pragmatic political thinking in the knowledge that the report will not be implemented anyway, they agreed to do the dirty deal and in the process neutralised further international efforts to criminalise Israeli and Hamas felonies. True, they woke up to the fact that they had committed an egregious error, and tried to put the clock back in a shabby démarche, but it was too late already and the Palestinian street had witnessed another shady political spin.

Moral pressure for change

But on 18 November 2009, the Rev Dr Samuel Kobia, General Secretary of the Geneva-based World Council of Churches, added his moral weight by urging UN Secretary-General Ban Ki-moon to ensure that the recommendations of this key report are properly followed up. He wanted the UN to press both Israel and Hamas to "unconditionally concede the need for complete and credible investigations into their actions during the war".

He cited "growing anxiety" that there could be a resolution that dilutes the intent and scope of the Goldstone Report, and added that durable peace, reconciliation and healing between Palestinians and Israelis should be based on justice since the need of the hour is an unequivocal affirmation of the highest principles of justice, human rights and humanitarian practices. It seems ironic that the WCC member-churches understood the significance of such a report, whilst the Palestinian leadership misunderstood its impact due to extrinsic pressures.

Another nail in the coffin was the Palestinian idea to proclaim a Rhodesia-style UDI – a unilateral declaration of independence – that would ostensibly be supported by the West let alone the Arab League. But not only had Yasser Arafat already made a similar declaration in 1988 to little effect, it was clear that such a move now will have spurred Israel to act unilaterally against it and also blurred EU or US support further. Were there no political advisers, or even Palestinian general delegates in the West, who could have admonished the leadership against Saeb Erekat's anachronistic public statement?

Clearing the ground

Today, in the midst of a Palestinian near-meltdown, the people are owed a degree of honesty, humility, consensus-building and clarity from all their leaders, and the present faces across the whole political spectrum fall short of fulfilling many of those attributes. Meanwhile, Israel busies itself erecting a fortress-like settlement in Jabal Abu Ghneim / Har Homa on the outskirts of Bethlehem, and establishing Jewish neighbourhoods in the heart of Sheikh Jarrah, Silwan, Ras al-Amud and Abu Dis. Parallel to this, and as Uri Avnery indicated in one of his recent articles, Israel is also trying to fill up the E1 area between Jerusalem and the settlement of Ma'aleh Adumim in order to encircle the Arab quarters and cut them off from the West Bank. By enlarging Jerusalem to the East up to the approaches of Jericho, Israel aims to cut the West Bank into two, with the northern part (Ramallah, Nablus, Jenin, Tulkarem) sawn off from the southern part (Bethlehem, Hebron).

I recall the Israeli hard-line foreign minister, Avigdor Lieberman, once stating that "anyone who says that within the next few years an agreement can be reached ending the conflict simply does not understand the situation and spreads delusions." Yet, within the orbit of this conflict, nothing has riled Palestinians or frustrated their irenic intentions more than the continued flow of illegal Israeli settlers into East Jerusalem and the West Bank as they gobble up the geography of an already shrunken future Palestinian statelet under a package of pretexts – from religious zealotry to political expansionism.

Indeed, this has become more of a red flag at the moment than even the future of Jerusalem or the return of refugees since they too are dependent upon geography to house demography. After all, both Oslo (1993) and the Road Map (2003) called for settlements to stop, but the number of settlers has instead risen steadily to over 450,000 today. That is also why, at 250 miles long, the wall-style barrier (projected to stretch over 400 miles once complete) is already much longer than the pre-1967 border or Green Line. And at a time when the West celebrated the 20th anniversary of bringing down the Berlin Wall, this ugly structure snaking across the West Bank places major settlements on the Israeli side, effectively annexing a further 12% of Palestinian land. How could anybody claim that Palestinians stand a chance of reversing this trend when any good faith necessary for achieving a resolution of the conflict remains absent from most regional or international key players?

Am I being a tad too pessimistic, or bluntly too realistic? I think perhaps the latter, and so I would suggest that the peace train has passed us by for now and we have to wait for a new generation with fresh impetus toward peace. In order to catch up with the train, we should learn not only to cast blame on our enemies who checkmate us, or on our allies who pursue their own vested interests, but we should also try to focus on our own weaknesses and redundancies. Perhaps in order to salvage Palestine, we should first salvage Palestinians – essentially their leaderships – so that the approach to this conflict is one that does not allow a spherical football to arrest the attention of a region whilst the future of a whole people is at stake.

Fatah today is a 50-year-old middle-aged movement, and it started its introspection, re-building as much as re-legitimising – almost its re-definition – in August 2009 with the General Conference in Bethlehem. Yet, it still has to define further its political purpose and national project let alone its organic relationship with the PA and with Hamas. To this end, it will have to agree upon the political space that will be shared between those two movements – and more importantly, how? After all, Hamas has to draw back from the precipice too and not allow its positive power to become a negative force that destroys the very cause that its leadership constantly tells us it defends – presumably for the sake of all Palestinians, be they Christian or Muslim, in the West Bank, Jerusalem or Gaza. Otherwise, it will turn into a movement that is antithetical to Palestine.

Looking for alternatives

But meanwhile, what is the alternative? Are we coming closer to embracing popular resistance and armed struggle (al-moukawama al wataniyya) as the only option still available to Palestinians? I do not think that this is the right option either, since it has shown its moral failing, political limitations and military shortcomings during the two past *Intifadas* – and most certainly during the second one. Instead, I would suggest that the world community – including Palestinian leaders in Gaza and the West Bank – sit down and re-read the National Conciliation Document of the Prisoners that came out on 28 June 2006 from an agreement negotiated in jail between representatives of the two leading Palestinian factions. Therein lies one answer for a format of national consensus at this critical juncture of the conflict. In fact, what could be more appropriate than a refresher course on the contents of this document at the very time that an exchange of

Palestinian-Israeli prisoners could well take place very soon and end up re-positioning the likes of Marwan Barghouti on the political landscape? But even breathing life into a three-year-old document is not enough either: looking at the history of other liberation movements, I realise that Palestinians continue to see-saw between violence and passivity, and they should perhaps also consider embracing a little more robustly and systematically the culture of non-violent resistance to an Israeli political leadership – not necessarily representative of its entire people – that encroaches further upon Palestinian rights, freedoms and lands.

Hearing the voice of the voiceless
I believe that the future hopes of Palestinians appear grim unless they shift gears and edge forward in a more cohesive way forward. But will their leaders, as well as much of the Arab World or the West, allow them to pursue their aspirations? Or will they simply remain faithful to the process of taking one step forward and two steps backward – and in the process losing out every time? When will the voice of the voiceless no longer remain muffled but become audible and challenging?

24 November 2009

Chapter 17

Religion, philosophy and Israel–Palestine

"It's the same world as the one into which Jesus came – in so many ways a place that can drive us to despair or rage, and yet now and forever a world in which God is real so that neither rage nor despair can be the only or ultimate option for us." – Dr Rowan Williams (then Archbishop of Canterbury, Amman, Jordan, February 2010)

I would like to reprise my Middle Eastern odyssey today by juxtaposing those inspiring words of faith from a theist of deep conviction and outreach with the belief system of Jean-Paul Sartre, perhaps the ultimate atheist and celebrity philosopher. In one sense, both men hold out for me a same note of encouragement toward peace-seeking and non-violence in Israel–Palestine, or – for that matter – throughout a broad region that is riven with violence, hatred, injustice, discrimination, corruption, nepotism and wars. After all, Sartre was a man who provided the French people with some direction and hope during the Second World War – not unlike Dr Rowan Williams in the midst of so much more recent uncertainty, diffidence and fear.

Beyond a narrow identity

It has been written that Sartre's existentialism addressed the dangers of allowing oneself to get trapped in the past, weighted under a whole slew of positive or negative expectations, and that he underlined his belief in the corresponding need to take personal responsibility for the future. This idea of freedom, of stepping out boldly beyond the confines of one's narrowly defined identity with its exogenous parameters, was a political manifesto as much as a philosophical creed. Dr Williams's ethos also steers people in the direction of liberating oneself from a past of rage and despair and moving faithfully toward the future – in other words, not to be beholden to the angst of the past but to labour for the promise of better times.

For me, one major difference between the one-time Archbishop of Canterbury and J-P Sartre though is that the former happens to be a man of mature Christian faith as well as nominal leader of 77 million Anglicans worldwide, while the latter was someone who had drifted away from his maternal Catholicism although he still retained enormous influence in France till his death in 1980, as he highlighted the constant interplay between an inherited 'facticity' that forms us and a 'freedom' that takes us into a heretofore inexistent future.

I am neither a philosopher nor a theologian, more of an independent legal politician, but I believe that both men encourage people to move forward rather than stay shackled to the past. I would even venture to add that Sartre's famous *L'enfer, c'est les autres* in the play *Huis clos* is tantamount to a political meditation on the ill-effects of living in what we call today a surveillance society that is dramatised by insufferable oppression and overweening vanity.

Why do I introduce J-P Sartre and Archbishop Williams into my Israeli-Palestinian reflections? Perhaps it is a cheeky response to my increasing frustration at the inability of failing politicians to go to a place where rage and despair are no longer the ultimate option, but where they could discover a future that is not incandescent with bitter memories or insuperable checkpoints. I find it harder every year to lay the blame for the political stasis in the region – including that in Israel–Palestine – on global influences alone rather than on a lack of fresh political vision that could couple itself with good will for peace.

The future overtakes the past?

So what about Israel–Palestine in recent years as one case of the future overtaking the past? It is quite obvious that Palestinians are in dire. The Palestinian Authority remains seriously discredited despite its hollow attempts – and those of other countries like Egypt – to revive its credibility after the hard blows it sustained in the recent past; not least following its unsuitable reaction to the Goldstone Report saga.

Moreover, and encouraged initially by no less than President Obama's demand from Israel for a full freeze on settlements, it is now left even more powerless since the US Administration has singularly failed to achieve anything more substantive than oratorical or rhetorical displays. President Obama seems to have almost yielded to Israeli *diktats* for the sake of his domestic and foreign policy considerations. Hence his abandonment of the pre-condition of a settlement freeze and the adoption of the already tested and failed proximity talks as a way of elongating the negotiations whilst aborting any tangible results.

With Hamas sniping at the legitimacy of the Authority, despite the fact that it is marginalised in Gaza and faces serious geopolitical challenges, PA President Abbas finds himself on a political tree unable to climb down with any half-decent face-saving formula. I applaud his irenic intentions, but his mandate has been characterised with manifold errors or misjudgements that have negated democracy, good governance and secular politics and have led many people to question his penchant for going the extra mile with Israel – leading to an accrual of extra miles that together have left Palestinians with hardly any territory, and with a sense of hybrid nationalism that neither feeds hungry babies nor restores any sense of dignity and pride.

Facing this Palestinian evanescent dream is a hapless US administration that is a wonderful gift for the current Israeli government as its troika implements vicious right-wing policies on an occupied land that is not its own anyway. So vicious in fact that it does not even refer to occupation anymore as the source of the conflict when dealing with the 1967 territories but instead turns the whole issue on its head by claiming that the occupation is actually helping combat terror! The Israeli truism suggests that any relinquishment of land to Palestinians would clearly weaken the so-called "war on terror". How suitable for Israeli expansionism, but equally how sad for world opinion – for us in the EU, for many Arab states and for much of the US – that accepts the oppression visited upon Palestinians as a quid pro quo for an amorphous global security.

It baffles me that a whole stable of regional experts in those world capitals that matter – and those that do not matter either – have not cottoned on to the fact that the Israeli-Palestinian conflict (1) remains the skeleton key to any peace in the whole region despite the sophistry of all contrary arguments, and (2) that it is a wasted and unproductive effort to spend time fighting Syria, Hizbullah or Hamas when the whole point is that Syria and those two resistance movements are viewed by a huge number of the pan-Arab populace as the sole true proponents of their inherent rights – against corrupt, authoritarian, money-hungry and oil-friendly Arab regimes and their foreign backers alike.

When American, Israeli and Arab state policies continue to dehumanise and dismiss the ordinary Arab in the street, it does not require a genius with a degree in political science to conclude that those peoples would strongly resent their oppressors and those supporting them or are allied with them. Convinced of Western double-standards, and the impotence of their regimes, they dig in their heels against further injustice, seeking self-protection in those core values that are sometimes viewed as regressive Islamist, extremist and violent.

Living in the shadows

Yet, do Israel and the US truly appreciate this reality, and understand the shadow it is casting on the efforts of many peacemakers? After all, Israel (or the spoilt child of the Middle East, as the Saudi Foreign Minister described it recently), pursues apace its apartheid and colonial policies with arrogant impunity, correctly calculating that, regardless of Prime Minister Netanyahu's lack of chemistry with President Obama, the US would not jeopardise the bilateral strategic relationship with Israel in the face of the Iranian nuclear issue. Only recently [February 2010], Israel stated its plans to build another 600 homes in occupied Arab East Jerusalem, near the Pisgat Ze'ev and Shu'fat neighbourhoods.

There are now roughly 200,000 settlers 'squatting' in the greater Jerusalem area, with the number of settlers in the West Bank having quadrupled from about 78,000 in 1990 to around 300,000 in 2009. This is not only a demographic issue: it also wreaks havoc with any hope for a future independent, viable and contiguous Palestinian state. As far back as 1988, PLO Chairman Yasser Arafat had predicted the establishment of a Palestinian sovereign state within two years. Yet today, 22 years later, that prediction remains a distant unreality and the peace process has become an offensive façade. America continues to bankroll Israeli policies that undermine its strategic objectives and render the whole region less safe – a Congressional Research Service stated that US aid to Israel totalled $28.9 billion over the past decade – and the Arab World busies itself with summit meetings and compulsive communiqués.

But what about the EU, our own club of 28 member-states, you might ask? One unusually blunt – albeit much-edited – statement earlier this year criticised Israeli settlements, the 'separation barrier' and the demolition of Palestinian homes, adding that they were "illegal under international law, constitute an obstacle to peace and threaten to make a two-state solution impossible." It also reminded all concerned that the EU "has never recognized the annexation of East Jerusalem."

In some sense, this pan-European statement might well be the most meaningful development since the Venice Declaration of 13 June 1980. However, the fact remains that the EU – whether as a collective body or individual states – is still unable to translate its financial and moral support to Palestinians under occupation into genuine political impulse. It needs to decouple its foreign policy from that of the USA long enough to deal with the conflict proactively and help tailor a resolution that would incidentally also serve our European interests. Otherwise, its gestures – whether over the import of agricultural products from settlements or its cost-free perorations – will remain mere whimpers in the face of a roaring regional calamity.

Spurious pretexts

Global terror is admittedly a menace today, but it is not a genetic Middle Eastern and Arab one. Most Arabs are not terrorists, just as most Palestinians are not rabid Israel–haters and most Muslims are not blood-curdling fanatics. This should not need saying, but it does. Global terror results from a mutation of different conditions ranging from military occupation to political oppression and consequential economic penury. Is it not high time that politicians stop using pretexts to 'justify' their immobility let alone their reluctance to act decisively?

It is self-evident that Palestinians should get their own house in order – a herculean task given their current fragmentation and animosities – and they should also be more inclusive of Israel as a lasting reality, but let us not hoodwink everyone by hiding behind spurious pretexts and conveniently overlooking that Yitzhak Rabin and Yasser Arafat shook hands on the south-side of the White House lawn in 1991 with the PLO charter to destroy Israel still intact. Things change through negotiation, not necessarily through bombs or militarisation or side-talks. After all, if we are ready to engage Taliban elements in Afghanistan today, could we not also think a bit more laterally in the case of the Israeli-Palestinian conflict too? Or has the political imagination of our leaders become so insular that they create ethical excuses to justify unethical inertia as they pick and choose their friends and foes at the expense of Palestinian lives, hopes and wishes?

Engaging the future

Jean-Paul Sartre and Archbishop Rowan Williams – perhaps ideological antipodes – understood this transparent truth, encouraging us to overstep our narrow realities and engage with the future. So my challenge to politicians and actors in the Israel–Palestine drama is for them to mull over an ancient Roman saying: *Tempus edax, homo edacior* ("Time destroys, man destroys more") in the hope that they might – just – prove Victor Hugo wrong.

27 February 2010

Chapter 18

Obama was in Israel

Prior to President Barack Obama's headline visit to Israel (March 2013), alongside those to Palestine and Jordan, one key question asked by many observers was whether he would pull a rabbit out of his hat and come up with some formula to move the Israeli-Palestinian negotiations on, and help nudge both sides with a process for peace (since it was never truly a peace process) that has been crawling forward and then hurriedly sliding backward time and again for at least two decades.

I always maintained that this was the wrong question and certainly the wrong expectation. President Obama came to Jerusalem for a different set of priorities. One primary aim was to win over the Israeli public to the fact that he was as staunch a defender of Israel as any other president ever since the creation of the state in 1948. In fact, he not only achieved this objective but also surpassed himself with all the emoting, back-slapping and over-enthusiastic endorsements of Israel and its history since the period of the Dead Sea Scrolls that date back to at least 200 BCE. He even achieved an American presidential first by visiting Theodor Herzl's grave, the founder of Zionism at the First Congress in Basle in 1897.

Naming the rights of Palestinians

His other politically less emotive but more cerebral priorities – which could have been done over the phone, incidentally – included serious and perhaps robust discussions with the Israeli prime minister over the Iran nuclear file, the gory violence in Syria, the politics of flux in Egypt and the intractable Israel–Palestine conflict. I have no idea what went on in private, since the public statements were so well choreographed that they gave a new flair to the definition of coordination.

However, on the Israeli-Palestinian conflict, President Obama delivered a compelling talk to a group of Israeli young men and women (including non-Jews) in Binyenei HaUma (International Convention Center) at Giv'at Ram in Jerusalem. His talk was vintage Obama in that it was professorial, oratorical, glib and political at one and the same time. And once we had moved past the first half of the talk that dripped with overflowing acclaim for Israel and its right to exist on this land, it was actually quite moving in recalling the rights of Palestinians for justice and peace in an independent and viable state.

Disgruntled as the Palestinian and Jordanian public were with their perceptions of a biased visit, this talk might well have touched a raw nerve. After all, the time the president spent in Ramallah, Bethlehem (via the ugly separation wall) or Amman and Petra was almost incidental to the main focus on Israel. But to its credit, the US Administration also offered Jordan $200 million to assist with the Syrian refugee problem that is snapping the back of an ailing Jordanian economy.

But what about this talk to young men and women? Where does it rate on the political Richter scale?

I followed the feedback not only on television and radio or in the written press but also on Twitter and the larger blogosphere. Many people were positive, even congratulatory, of the talk and the rare way it sliced through equivocation. Quite, but I have never doubted President Obama's elocution, linguistic abilities and intelligence or even his proclivity to season his talks with Hebrew words when describing Israel as *Eretz Nehederet* (a wonderful land) that is a throwback to a popular TV satire show. What I have seriously doubted though is his willingness to act upon those skills in order to coerce – not merely cajole – Israeli politicians into making those peacemaking concessions that a majority of the Israeli public seemingly supports according to successive polls.

Israel and the arc of justice

However, I am loath to disappoint Palestinians and Jordanians further by asserting that I see no real proof whatsoever that Israeli governmental trends will alter in any concrete way. The talks might well continue as they have done throughout the past two decades since the Madrid conference of 1991, the Oslo Accords of 1993, the Geneva Accord of 2003, the rejection by Israel of the Arab Peace Initiative of 2002 (reaffirmed by the League of Arab States in 2009), the Abbas-Olmert / Livni discussions in 2008 let alone the personal initiatives or injudicious promises that have been not only disappointments but also deceptions – in short, political sleights of hand.

At one level, hope is an abstract notion, and hope solely in an America-tailored and enforced settlement today is nothing more than a chimera. The Israelis and Palestinians will only manage to draw nearer to a peaceful resolution of the conflict if Israel acknowledges that it is occupying and colonising another people on their land – Dead Sea

Scrolls notwithstanding in the real world – and desist from applying those oppressive measures that are apartheid-like. But hand-in-hand with an Israeli lack of obfuscation and procrastination would come a Palestinian acceptance to forgo some treasured chestnuts in return for an internationally-brokered peace. Can either side pull it off now? No. *Ergo,* the USA will not pull its weight, the conflict will not be resolved any time soon and the creeping settlements will render a two-state solution well nigh impossible, with the one-state alternative remaining unacceptable to Israel. It will eventually boil down to demography, to the long-term consequences of the Arab uprisings and to the political backbone of new Arab leaders.

One of President Obama's favourite quotations comes from the civil rights campaigner Martin Luther King Jr. that, "The arc of the moral universe is long, but it bends toward justice." It seems to me the arc is unendingly long for our lifetime. Oh, I forget, there was also a clearly significant – even strategic – achievement for President Obama: a call between Prime Ministers Benyamin Netanyahu and Recep Tayyip Erdoğan laid to rest the tiff between Israel and Turkey over the Mavi Marmara incident of 2010. A shame though that he did not pull off a similar call between Netanyahu and Abbas.

25 March 2013

Chapter 19

Prayers and politics for Israelis and Palestinians

During his whistle-stop tour of Amman, Bethlehem and Jerusalem last month, Pope Francis invited Presidents Shimon Peres and Mahmoud Abbas to join him at the Vatican. "I offer my home in the Vatican as a place for this encounter of prayer", he stated, and the key question that has been on the minds of many ecumenical commentators is whether there is more to this impromptu invitation than mere prayer between a Christian host and his Jewish and Muslim guests.

I believe that Pope Francis is indeed inviting both leaders for 'a heartfelt prayer' on 8 June 2014 in the hope that it might well help soften some of the hardened hearts or tackle the mounting cynicism that surrounds any renewed discussion over the festering Israeli-Palestinian conflict. After all, I would quite reasonably posit that it did not take this Pope too long – whether from what he saw with his own eyes or heard with his own ears – to realise that Palestinians are an occupied people thirsting for freedom, dignity and space in order to found a state that they too could proudly call their home.

It is quite true that the Pope's visit both to Bethlehem and Jerusalem was a masterly exercise in symmetry. The position of the Holy See has always been consistent on the Israeli-Palestinian conflict, but this pope who thrives on personal contacts did not want either party to criticise him for being partisan. Yet, his roots as a Latin American church leader who is familiar with the whole movement of liberation theology would normally help him empathise with the underdog and the vulnerable in any society. No wonder he stopped unexpectedly in front of the ugly Separation Wall in Bethlehem. No wonder too that he matched this gesture with an equal one in Jerusalem ostensibly at the behest of the Israeli Prime Minister. The message had been sent out. "I hear you", he said to Palestinians' "but there is so much I can do personally".

This explains to some extent his invitation to Peres and Abbas that takes place on a major feast – Pentecost Sunday – for Christians worldwide. No wonder too that Pope Francis extended his Invocation for Peace to Ecumenical Patriarch Bartholomew I and other religious leaders to join him for prayer and meditation with the two presidents.

After all, this Eastern Orthodox Church leader is primus inter pares – first among equals – within the hierarchy of the Orthodox Church. Orthodox Palestinians – and Arabs – form a majority of Christians in the Holy Land and in the broader MENA region.

But what will those prayers do to a conflict whose competing narratives are first and foremost political?

Not too much in my opinion! And frankly, I do not think that Pope Francis expects a sudden transformation that would unshackle the hearts of Israeli or Palestinian political leaders who would then rush headlong into a 'comprehensive' deal.

However, the Pope is also acutely aware of the opinion, feedback and positions of the Palestinian churches in the Holy Land let alone of those men, women and children he met during his recent trip to Amman, Bethlehem and Jerusalem.

I believe that the Israeli-Palestinian political impasse is primarily the result of an Israeli occupation of Palestinian lands since 1967. A long-standing occupation has been bleeding the Palestinian psyche dry and emasculating its daily realities. The inexorable colonisation of Palestinian land and the concomitant 'settlemania' in Jerusalem or the West Bank are not only grabbing lands and in so doing flouting International law. They are also shifting the demographics of this small parcel of land and rendering a much-mooted 'two-state' solution increasingly more impracticable. The spin of an incumbent Israeli PM, who is being aided and abetted by a coterie of hard-line ministers, has reached such incalculable proportions that many Palestinians – and certainly the new generations who have never known anything else – are almost too familiar with such a corrosive occupation that is gobbling up their human and national rights.

Have Palestinians been their worst enemies too? Of course, since power-plays are often a feature of most societies that are not 'democratic' – in other words, those that are not in control of their own destinies. But Palestinian divisions cannot be an egress for Israeli culpability. With an Israeli cabinet that refuses to discuss peace whether Hamas are in the fold or outside it, and with an international community that puts up disingenuously with the spins coming out of 3 Kaplan Street in Jerusalem (PM Benyamin Netanyahu's office), even the most dovish Palestinian president – and Abu Mazen is such a dove – cannot deliver the goods.

Having worked with the ecumenical movement on second-track negotiations, I know they are often helpless – and even clueless at times

– in helping resolve political conflicts. Perhaps Archbishop Emeritus Desmond Tutu is one of the few towering exceptions to this rule. However, I have also come to respect the humbling moral authority some religious leaders bring with them. And this cannot be truer than for Francis who is not only the head of 1.2 billion Catholic Christians but is also marshalling his Petrine moral integrity to encourage the two ageing presidents to inch forward in their quest for peace.

The two presidents in the Vatican on 8th June might not be the men to pen an agreement that frees Palestinians from the yoke of oppression while also providing security for Israelis. But with them, the message that Pope Francis is emitting targets the political establishment in Jerusalem well before Ramallah. Bluntly put, if Israel does not wish to end up facing a binational / one state-solution that dwarfs its own Jewish identity, it might as well grasp – belatedly – this olive branch! The alternative is not for more walls in hearts, minds and lands, but alas for more bitterness and inescapable violence.

8 June 2014

Chapter 20

Vox populi for a changing political world

It is really James Abbott's fault! James is someone I have had the honour of working with through the Catholic Bishops Conference of England and Wales. He has often invited me into his studio for interviews on issues relating to the Middle East and North Africa region for the *Middle East Analysis* series of podcasts. He has also encouraged me to make more use of Twitter and other social media to reach the global constituency.

Now, politics and diplomacy for me (as I use them quite interchangeably) are two skills that I had learnt the hard way over many years of second-track negotiations – essentially between Israel and the Palestinians, but also between Greek and Turkish Cypriot islanders, or else in the more byzantine and less predictable maze of church politics.

It consisted, frankly, of the art of communication, negotiation, mediation, arbitration and alternative dispute resolution, but it also consisted of an abundance of notes, memos and position papers or else the rather enjoyable meetings over lunches and dinners and even the more frugal coffees with the occasional *narguilehs* and cigars under my all-time favourite cumquat tree in the very heart of Jerusalem.

This was the art of 'politicking' or 'lobbying' or 'talking' in order to find solutions, defuse crises – real or potential – and to set out agendas for the future. Little did it occur to me at a time when I had become addicted to the heady ways of high-powered powwows, discussions, initiatives and business-class travels, that such efforts would soon witness a radical shift across the Middle East and North Africa spectrum and also necessitate an equal Newtonian change in me and other interlocutors.

Out of the diplomatic enclave

Discomfiting? Perhaps a little. Out of the blue? Not really. After all, those who set policies or took decisions and tweaked realities – whether in secular society or (perhaps especially) in the religious life – often represented very few people other than themselves. Democracy for them largely meant that it was 'their way or the highway' since elections – if they ever took place in this ancient part of the world – were theatrical and people in the MENA region were not used to the idea of expressing their choices or their preferences through the ballot box.

But with the outbreak of the so-called Arab Spring over two years ago, when masses of men, women and even children began swarming the public squares and clamouring for dignity, essential freedoms and economic justice, those established rules of political life began teetering precariously – more in some countries than in others. The Facebook and Twitter generations suddenly took to the streets in protest and at times paid with their lives (they sadly still do so today) in order to undo the shackles of oppression from misrule or corruption and become responsibly proud citizens of their own countries rather than human beings at the call and behest of autocratic or totalitarian rulers.

But all this spontaneity in freedom-struggling was never going to be easy or straightforward. We know – or can at least predict – the story if we also know the dominant cultures of the Middle East and North Africa region a little bit. After all, every reader of this article will probably have followed to some degree the unfolding of those grassroots movements. These young people – the *vox populi* as they were quaintly described by the media back then, having now been converted into 'tweeps' – were stealthily sidetracked and marginalised by the better-organised and well-funded interest groups who had not initially been expecting this regional outburst but who were all too willing to take credit for it and then steer social movements in their own preferred directions.

So damaging forms of politics and religion came together alongside corrupt rulers and self-interested military cadres to regain, once more, the lost ground and re-establish the *status quo* ante under a different guise, in order to row back toward a supposedly happy mix of personal hedonism and unquestionable rule among an emerging middle class, for instance.

But social networking nevertheless continued to thrust itself to the foreground, and state television channels as much as politicians, religious leaders and diplomats could no longer readily preach hackneyed and jaundiced messages that lifted up the 'rulers' and put down the masses without being challenged and called to account. Democracy, denied by the region's rulers, was now being rediscovered technologically by ordinary people in houses and streets across the region. It was a tool of empowerment, shifting the balance of power away from autocrats.

So welcome to the fresh world in the broader Middle East and North Africa (MENA) region, where social media and digital diplomacy, already exercised by ambassadors, politicians and parliamentarians, as well as by the Pope (believe it or not), has been displacing the previously unchallenged opinions of longstanding observers and remote intellectuals. This digital revolt signifies openness as much as an understanding, while of on-the-ground realities that have heretofore been hidden or (mis)represented behind dense smokescreens of propaganda suddenly find a global as well as a local audience, with mainstream media needing to negotiate a wider range of sources and viewpoints.

The new digital hand on reality

In this way a top-down political pyramid was slowly re-discovering its base, and new digital media resources are still being spawned from every corner. While writing this, for example, I discovered *Syria Deeply,* one of many Google+ hangouts that bring the political kaleidoscope of Syria straight onto viewers' screens. I am now living this experience in a modest way, as I broaden my political work across a large swathe of the MENA region. Discussing politics with a few people over a brandy is definitely anachronistic today if one truly wishes to understand the region by touching the political heartbeat or feeling the cultural pulse of people on the streets.

No amount of top-down diplomacy, meetings at the EU in Brussels or conclaves in churches can translate the true picture of what is happening in Israel–Palestine and the MENA region to any inquisitive mind. In Syria, to use one example, I have benefited from messages coming from front-line activists talking about events inside a country that is often not accessible or hospitable to the mainstream media. Otherwise, how would I know almost instantly that Syria is trying to create diversions by sending tanks into the demilitarised zone of the Golan Heights, when it had not fired a single bullet toward Israel for four decades? How would I gauge the reaction of Syrian men and women inside the country to the newly-formed opposition coalition with Ahmed Moadh Khatib, Riad Seif, Suhair Atassi or George Sabra?

Where else would I get byte-by-byte accounts of the detention of the Bahraini activist Nabeel Rajab and then gauge the reaction on the street? Would I hear about the gaoled netizen Sattar Beheshti as he was interrogated and later died at the Evin prison in Iran? Or else that

Hakem al-Mutairi, an Islamist who wrote an article 'undermining' the Emir's status ten years ago, was called by Kuwait's public prosecutor for interrogation?

If I were to rely solely on my 'official' or 'ecumenical' sources, would I learn the real story behind the Christian divisions in Syria amongst those supporting the regime, the majority of whom are fearfully sitting on the fence, or of those who are offering their lives in order to effect change? Would I be stuck in a time warp that parrots the mantra of multi-faith leaders whose messages on behalf of the regime are disingenuous at best and counter-productive at worst.

In Palestine I can now use digital tools to learn the opprobrium felt by ordinary men and women about their own leadership – be it in Gaza or the West Bank – and the way they export messages that subsequently become part of a new online diplomacy. The case for Palestinian self-determination that has been built up brick-by-brick and sweat-by-sweat by Christians and Muslims alike is being inexorably eroded by a pernicious occupation only equalled by the insidious interests of those leaders who live in their insular citadels and spew out religious radicalism on the one hand and political spam on the other. Can the contradictory signals of digitised reality bring people together and create stronger mass movements to effect change? Will they enable or confuse? Probably both.

What I say about Syria, Bahrain or Palestine applies across the whole MENA region, of course. Be it in Egypt, Lebanon, Jordan, Morocco, Tunisia, the GCC countries or elsewhere, new and furious voices are being heard. An ambassador living in Rabat or Cairo can still listen to a foreign minister coming out with the official position of the regime, but can then canvass reactions from the street before sending an encrypted analysis to his or her bosses. In Oman, some politicians log on the Sabla chat-room every morning to get a sense of the street before they start their working days.

Given these developments, I am not surprised to detect the dissent bubbling under the surface in many Middle East and North Africa countries that have not yet reeled from the uprisings. After all, those ructions we witness today are both multi-seasonal and long-term. As the syndicated journalist Rami Khouri often reminds his readers, it took long periods for the French, English and American revolutions to bear fruit. If the previous rulers of the MENA region – from Zine al-Abidine Ben Ali and Ali Abdullah Saleh to Hosni Mubarak, Muammar Qadhafi and Bashar Al-Assad – had listened to those increasingly desperate grassroots murmurs and had supported institutional change, we might perhaps not be witnessing so much of the tragic violence we see today.

Rediscovering the voice of the people

If the other rulers in the region (or even outside it) also take a moment to listen to those audible murmurs, the *vox populi* and tweeps, they might save themselves darker fates, too. What would be wonderful would be if social media sharing rather than violence could be harbingers for real peace.

A different approach to diplomacy ought to be the natural result of those who truly want to listen to the messages of the people coming out of the MENA region – messages that challenge many of the regular tropes about politics, religion and culture. In a region with "fingerprints of fire but footprints of peace" (to use the title of Noel Moules' admirable book) it is a mammoth task looking at each situation afresh from multiple angles.

There is also the pressing need for verification and validation, given that technology can be used to distort as well as reveal. And of course extremist groups can also make extensive use of the digital revolution, as well as civic groups and peacemakers. There are huge challenges still to negotiate. But the genie cannot be put back in the bottle. The diverse voice of the people is here to stay, and monolithic political structure will have to change.

11 November 2012

Part Five: Resisting Despair

Prologue

Resisting despair is a double-edged task. It entails identifying the things that drag us down or oppress us, and finding ways of not being bowed by them; ways of standing in solidarity. It also involves discovering and exploring the sources of hope and magnifying them as much as we can. Much of this book has been about politics, diplomacy and civic action in Israel–Palestine. Here we start with a meditation (chapter twenty-one) on Christmas – the place where, for Christians, the incarnation of love, justice and peace stands in contrast to he malign spirit of occupation – and where stillness rather than violence reigns. Of course, in a divided context, hope for some can be despair for others. That, too, must be faced. Chapter twenty-two, written in 2006, explores the Palestinian *nakba* in detail, suggesting at the end that a reframing of the mindset can assist on the path to progress and change. Resistance and hope, hand in hand, are not abstract but historical. This is brought out in chapter twenty-three, with a striking but sobering snapshot of the Middle East (including Palestine), once again connecting to the Christmas quest for peace. Solidarity and togetherness, as well as practical support for civic and faith communities under pressure, is a strong feature of the Holy Land Coordination outlined in chapter twenty-four (2016). The aim here is to illustrate how NGOs, churches and other groups can work together to nurture a constructive response to the challenges of the region. Chapters twenty-five and twenty-six, meanwhile, look at the dangers to a credible, just settlement that come from the sharp fork in US policy under Trump and the re-election of Netanyahu in Israel. Both articles, bringing the story tight up to date, end on a cautiously positive note. The political pendulum can and will swing. We must be ready.

Chapter 21

The stillness of Christmas in the Holy Land

Most of the Christmas 'celebrations' in Bethlehem, as much as other places in Palestine, have been cancelled for this season. This has been a regular pattern over the years, as the Separation Wall and occupation take their toll. What was meant to be a veritable pageantry of different shows that would have concluded the Jubilee year of 2000 has now become muted and noiseless. Most people are too sad, pre-occupied, jobless or bereft of hope, to indulge in the merriment that had become an annual trademark of this land – just like any other land elsewhere in the world. So has Christmas ended in the Holy Land? Not at all. Let me tell the story once more, from the cradle of Christianity. For it is our abiding hope.

First, in the midst of all the gloomy uncertainty in Israel Palestine (and elsewhere), it is important for people to recall that Christmas here is not a pagan celebration that manifests itself only with all manner of loud things such as geese, shepherds, drums, camels, crackers, the colours red and gold, angels, choirs, kings and pillar boxes. It is true that the consumerist mind associates Christmas with bells pealing, children shouting, the turkey sizzling, corks popping from bottles of wine, dogs barking, wassailers singing, and somewhere above in the empyrean the angelic zithers and trumpets going full tilt. But is that truly how we should understand the Season? Can the spiritual and religious significance of this day be swapped for short-term commercial satisfaction? And besides, what does Christmas say about Peace? And more to the point, what does it say about Stillness? Christians in the Holy Land embody a different reality of Christmas hope.

Second, let me share with you all a thirteenth-century carol that has been one of my all-time favourites:

> He came all so still
> There his mother was
> As dew in April
> That falleth on the grass
> He came all so still
> There his mother lay
> As dew in April
> That falleth on the spray.

The mystery of Christmas has been elegantly captured in this carol. It is one of stillness. Yet, a paradoxical stillness, a stillness that confounds us and sneaks up on us, even when we think we have never made so much noise. Every year, when everything is more or less done, that stillness will descend on us. We may easily imagine that something else has caused it. Perhaps (in some parts of the world) the snow is muffling all sound. Perhaps our own bone-tiredness, or even the absence of our neighbours, is creating the stillness. But it is not imagination that makes the silence of Christmas night and Christmas morning so peculiarly pregnant and deep. This stillness is a signal not of absence, but rather one of presence. Mind you, such stillness may not last long. After all, it is not peace! It is the silent announcement of a miracle about to happen, with our hearts being prepared for it. Emmanuel, God with us. Just like the dew falling in fact. Or, as people used to say when a sudden stillness fell in the middle of a conversation, like an angel passing, with his trumpet mute.

But the stillness of that special moment at Christmas invariably points the way to the Mystery of the Incarnation. And devoid of all trappings, it is the Incarnation that alone uplifts that stillness into a miracle.

By way of illustration – in his *Confessions,* St Augustine explains why only the Incarnation gives satisfaction. During his spiritual journey, he writes, he was greatly attracted by the philosophy of the Platonists. Studying their books, he found there much that was close in substance to the Christian Gospel. They seemed to know, without saying it as such, that "in the beginning was the Word, the Word was with God, and the Word was God". They understood that "the light shines in the darkness, and the darkness has not overcome it". They believed in the immaterial soul. But that God, the Word, "was made flesh and dwelt among us" – that is something he did not find in their books.

Again, St Augustine wrote, the Platonists accepted that the Word "was born not of blood nor of the will of the flesh nor of the will of man, but of God". But they did not say, with the great Gospel of John, that "he came unto his own, and his own received him not". Nor that "to all who received him, who believed in his name, to them he gave power to become children of God". That would have been too earthly for these philosophical idealists. They were, St Augustine wrote, like people who "from some wooded mountain-top see the land of peace, without being able to find the way there".

Indeed, we need the revelation to find the way. We cannot do it by ourselves. We can reach only the point where we 'see the land of peace, without being able to find a way there'. Especially in a post-modern age, Enlightenment values alone will not take us. Nothing but the Incarnation, God with us in the flesh, as St Augustine discovered, will do.

Folk religion or New Age philosophy will not take us where we need to go, either. At the end of the path, the revelation when it comes is incredible yet utterly familiar. We can point to a baby lying in a manger and say, "That is God. That is what God is like." God is nearer to us than we are to ourselves. This is the end of all our longing, the fulfilment of our dreams. This is an answer to our dearest wish. Hope is possible. And yes, love is possible too.

As we all draw inexorably nearer to the miracle of the Nativity, it might do us well to pause for a few minutes and to listen to that stillness made manifest in the Mystery of the Incarnation. A miracle is taking place, and we are part of that miracle! As such, we can perhaps deprive ourselves for one moment of all the worldly signs of rejoicing – tinsels, crackers and all – and seek instead an inner wholeness that meets its ultimate truth in the stillness of that one memorable night in Bethlehem. I wish you all a Holy Christmas: May its Incarnational Stillness Inspire Your Lives.

23 December 2000

Chapter 22

The Palestinian *nakba* – where to now?

"We must do everything to ensure that they [the Palestinians] never do return. The old will die and the young will forget." – David Ben Gurion, 18 July 1948

At midnight, on 14 May 2006, Israeli Jews celebrated the 58th anniversary of the creation of their State. But these Israel–wide joyous celebrations were also an occasion for Palestinians to recall that the birth of this state resulted in their own dispossession and destitution, when the combined Irgun-Haganah forces launched an offensive in April 1948 and drove the Palestinian people out of their lands. I know this not solely because I have read it in history books, but more so because my late grandfather recounted to me time and again his memories of bundling my grandmother and three daughters (including my mother) together in a car, leaving the family home, business and properties in Talbieh and fleeing to Beirut for a brief period before settling down in the eastern part of Jerusalem that was at the time part of Jordan.

Indeed, successive Palestinian refugees – Christian, Muslim or Druze – grow up hearing the stories of those final moments in Palestine, the hard decisions and the panic, as they also re-live the terrible consequences of those fateful weeks. Books have been written, lectures have been given, organisations have been set up to defend the rights of Palestinian refugees, absentees and returnees, and all this as a result of the birth of one nation and the death of another.

Jewish villages were built in the place of Arab villages. Nahlal arose in the place of Mahlul; Kibbutz Gvat in the place of Jibta; Kibbutz Sarid in the place of Huneifis; and KefarYehushua in the place of Tal al-Shuman. There is not a single place built in this country that did not have a former Arab population – Moshe Dayan, at Technion Haifa, 4 April 1969

Throughout 1948, as the State of Israel was delivered by the midwifery of the British Mandate, Jewish forces expelled thousands of Palestinians from their villages, towns and cities into Gaza, the West Bank, Lebanon, Syria, Jordan, Egypt and Iraq. Palestinian societies were uprooted from 418 towns and villages, and hundreds of thousands of others fled their homes – and political homeland – because they were afraid to stay behind or were intimidated from doing so by the invading forces.

My grandfather, every time he recalled his garden with its lemon tree and the [now useless] keys to his front door, rued his decision to run away. He felt with hindsight that he had perhaps let his family down, but his UN friends had advised him to do so, and the fear of terrible consequences if he were to stay put had made him take this drastic step that ultimately cast him and his family out for many years. This is true of many other families, some of them my relatives, who also fled with their title deeds and keys but precious little else because they were afraid for their lives.

Dispossession was the Jewish objective, since its Zionist project aimed to create a Jewish state by expunging it of the original inhabitants who had lived there for centuries. The creation of the state of Israel was at the heart of this cataclysmic event for Palestinians, and its manifold cultural, socio-economic and political repercussions have recombined – almost genetically – in the Palestinian psyche as a phenomenon that became known as the *nakba* (or catastrophe). It remains one of the intractable symptoms of the conflict between Arabs and Israelis.

Today, there is a Palestinian minority in Israel that totals around 20 per cent of the overall population, many of them internally displaced persons or "present absentees" – a contradictory appellation given to the nearly 200,000 Palestinian citizens of Israel whose properties were taken by Israel, making them refugees within their own country. Hillel Cohen's *The Present Absentee: The Palestinian Internal Refugees in Israel since 1948* is only one of many references on the subject. There are equally the Palestinians living under occupation in the West Bank as a result of the defeat of the Arab forces in the Arab-Israeli war of 1967 (also known as the *naksa,* or setback), but there are also refugees in camps across the whole Arab world – from Jordan and Lebanon to Egypt and Syria – who are a constant mnemonic of this immutable reality.

However, the *nakba* has come to symbolise for Palestinians not only a historical event that is still being reeled out. It is a present-day reality too – whether for those living in camps across the West Bank, Gaza and the Arab world, or those under occupation (a different kind of refugee status) in their ever-shrinking lands. One consequence of this original *nakba* has been the entrenchment of apartheid (essentially colonialist) structures that have manifested themselves in anti-Palestinian racism and xenophobia across Israeli generations. Facing this colossal concatenation of circumstances, past and present, Palestinians have assumed the unenviable role of Sisyphus in Greek mythology as they passed the task of pushing the stone from one movement to the other across generations.

> We must use terror, assassination, intimidation, land confiscation, and the cutting of all social services to rid the Galilee of its Arab population. – Israel Koening, in the Koening Report (Memorandum), 1975

History, it seems, is not such a good tutor since the *nakba*, with its original perfidies, is being acted out today in other ways across the whole land. Within Israel, the Palestinian minority is resisting such discrimination through proactive legal and political means, although there are also those who try to find a solution by denying or belittling their identity. There are also those Palestinians under occupation in the West Bank who are remorselessly being made refugees again by a concrete wall that is gradually encircling their lands and homes.

This wall has already created thousands of refugees and cordoned off tracts of occupied land. Judged as illegal by the International Court of Justice in The Hague, the wall has nonetheless turned West Bank cities (such as Qalqilya) into ghost towns, and cut off thousands of Palestinians from their homes and businesses. Then, there are the Palestinians in Gaza who are under a different kind of occupation despite the withdrawal of the Israeli Army since they have been massed into ghettoes and forbidden to travel or work – not unlike the way Jews were treated in Europe during the 18C – in order to act out the numerous vested political interests of other parties, or even as a result of sheer indifference to their plight.

Walls and *machsomot* (checkpoints) constructed by Israel's occupying forces, Jewish-only by-pass roads traversing Palestinian lands, uprooted Palestinian orchards and olive groves, demolished Palestinian homes that are replaced with new or expanded settlements, or even extra-judicial assassinations, all demonstrate clearly the continuing nature of the *nakba* that besets Palestinians today. In fact, the latest political echoes from Israel indicate a priority toward a convergence plan whereby Israel would withdraw from a number of West Bank settlements on the east side of the wall whilst firming up its hold on the large settlement blocs on the west side.

This, alongside any unilateral disengagement along mooted lines, would lead to the creation of Palestinian cantons across the West Bank and lead to the discontinuation of any Palestinian future homeland on the remaining 22 per cent of historical Palestine. A landmass that enjoys neither sovereignty nor contiguity cannot be considered a viable entity – far less a future state – and would scupper any credible chance for a negotiated two-state solution as set out in the (now almost defunct) roadmap for peace.

Yet, this is precisely what is being prescribed for Palestinians today. I regard this emerging scenario as one that not only stunts the legitimacy of historical memory but also the reality of political geography. Over the past few weeks alone, the policy of the international community for imposing sanctions upon a democratically elected Palestinian government is tantamount to the collective punishment of an occupied people – rather than of the occupier.

To add insult to injury, Israel has refused to remit to the Palestinian Authority its tax revenues. Such monies being withheld are actually necessary to help alleviate the occupation tactics of sanctions, curfews, closures and checkpoints that have ruined the Palestinian economy. As I have written or lectured in the recent past, I am one of those who distrust by instinct the Islamist political agenda of Hamas. I also deplore the lamentable – and pusillanimous – intra-Palestinian struggles (be they ideology-based or power-driven, with an outlook that is at times tethered to the use of violence). However, neither distrust of Hamas, nor distaste for intra-Palestinian tugs-of-war, justify in any way the punishment of a people whose legitimate aspirations have been pawned to different interests and coalitions. Even principled positions cannot yield to workable policies, but only foment humanitarian catastrophes, political chaos and domestic mayhem.

Everybody has to move, run and grab as many hilltops as they can to enlarge the settlements because everything we taker now will stay ours ... Everything we don't grab will go to them. – Ariel Sharon, to Tsomet Party, 15 November 1998

During the optimistic days following the Declaration of Principles and the protracted Oslo process, one major stumbling block at all levels of the negotiations remained the issue of Palestinian refugees. This is not only due to a sheer instinct for survival or even historical memory by either side, or for that matter solely one of clashing nationalisms. It is the refusal by one side – Israel – to re-insert in its collective psyche the chip that would reboot its memory to the roots of its creation some 58 years ago and help it access its responsibility. But is also a refusal by the Palestinian side to devise a solution that underlines the juridical principle of return for Palestinian refugees, and then brings it forward to an achievable reality that would be acceptable to Israel let alone to the refugees themselves.

All this surely means that grandstanding should give way to education, and that treating Palestinian refugees as men and women without rights in order to window-dress the 'Palestinian cause' is counterproductive – and in some political sense counter-intuitive too. Both sides must admit at long last that this issue – amongst many that need to be overcome in order to secure peace between two peoples – needs to be resolved one day.

Fifty-eight years have passed since the exodus of thousands of families from their homes, and generations of Palestinians have been consigned to refugee camps in neighbouring Arab countries. Wars, international resolutions and countless peace initiatives have endeavoured to put an end to the Palestinian experience of subjugation, suppression, violence and displacement. Marking the anniversary of the *nakba* involves a realisation that it was not just a tragic moment in the history of Palestinians, but that it touches upon the core of the struggle for Arab dignity, identity and justice in the face of enormous odds and daunting power. The *nakba* that is part and parcel of the Palestinian national memory is simultaneously one that has also contributed to the configuration of its national identity. Consequently, what is required is a paradigm that could shift those variables and lead to equal peace for Palestinians and Israelis alike, since the *nakba* as a 58-year reality is seamlessly tied to the conflict – and its unending tragedy – today.

20 May 2006

Chapter 23

Peace and goodwill unto the Middle East

This week, men, women and children in numerous Middle Eastern households – from Jordan, Syria and Lebanon, to Egypt, Palestine and the Gulf countries – will undoubtedly be caught up in the Yuletide spirit. They will hope for a more peaceful world in 2011 and wish for the welfare and happiness of kith and kin alike. But how realistic are those sanguine hopes, and how palpable are the prospects today for peace and stability in the Middle East? Or to paraphrase loosely the Dutch philosopher Spinoza, how brutal is the lack of peace in this region?

Since the end of a year is not the time for political pedantry or for philosophical sophistry, I will unburden the reader of too many facts or figures and will simply glaze over 2010 with a couple of key issues from Israel–Palestine and Iraq that – apart from the ongoing WikiLeaks saga – have tenaciously courted the headlines in the European media over the past year.

In Israel–Palestine, following a spate of unyielding negotiations, the consensus seems to be that peace between Israelis and Palestinians has now become even less achievable. The Israeli waves of settlements in Jerusalem and the West Bank are almost unstoppable. The expansion of the large settlements of Ma'ale Adumim, the Gush Etzion block, Beitar Illit and Modi'in Illit continues unabated whilst there is also a fierce growth in the smaller and more remote outposts such as Tapuach, Talmon, Ofra, Eli and Shiloh. Even the recent American "sweeteners' to Israel in the form of a US$3 billion security assistance package, diplomatic cover and advanced F-35 fighter aircraft have failed to coax Prime Minister Bibi Netanyahu to agree on a paltry 90-day settlement freeze that would help resume the stalled negotiations with Palestinians. Today, there are over 300,000 Israeli illegal settlers in the West Bank and 200,000 Israeli Jews living in East Jerusalem. When coupled with a 45% rise in home demolitions (according to UNRWA 2010 reports), the eviction of many Palestinians or the expropriation of acres of their arable lands, the season surely cannot feel too festive for many Palestinian Muslims or Christians.

Is it any wonder that the Hebrew University philosopher Moshe

Halbertal argued lucidly in a recent op-ed that the window for a two-state solution is closing rapidly and that the Palestinians will soon lose their right to a sovereign state? But if this were to happen, Israel will then permanently occupy the West Bank and end up with a one-state solution that will have inside its belly 2.5 million Palestinians without rights of citizenship, alongside 1.5 million Israeli Arabs who hail from al-Nakba of 1948. Can such a state exist peaceably without sliding down the road of apartheid or, worse, internal combustion? No wonder then that a number of Latin American states have lent their *de jure* – albeit clearly not de facto – recognition of Palestine as a way of circumventing a moribund peace process and helping Palestinians achieve their statehood.

Sadly though, Palestinians at times behave as their worst own enemies. Over the years, they have committed egregious errors – not least among themselves, as well as with Jordan and Lebanon. But no single people deserve homelessness, and the EU today by and large still supports the two-state solution despite its failure to qualify as a competent midwife for this ectopic pregnancy.

In Iraq, and putting all political shenanigans aside, one primary concern is the ostensibly deliberate targeting of Christians by extremist groups such as the Islamic State of Iraq that is allegedly linked to *al-Qa'eda*. Such attacks were occurring for a while already, but they became more vehement after the deadly attack on the Church of Our Lady of Salvation on 31st October 2010. In fact, the situation is getting increasingly unsafe for Christians – let alone for other small communities such as Yezidis and Sabean-Mandaeans – and one senses from the Iraqis themselves as much as from the Christmas messages of Pope Benedict XVI and Archbishop Rowan Williams of a looming threat to the very existence of those communities. This sombre reality was highlighted again last week when the UNHCR stated that Iraqi Christian numbers had shrunk to roughly 500,000 from 1.4 million just before 2003.

Bluntly put, those Iraqi Christians who have been an integral part of the fabric of Middle Eastern society for two millennia are now on the run. Some are heading for cover in Kurdish regions such as Qosh whilst others are leaving for Syria, Jordan and even Turkey or Lebanon. But violence, forced displacement, discrimination, marginalisation and neglect have shaken their belief in the authorities and it is no surprise that churches prudently cancelled many of their Christmas celebrations out of concern for their faithful. Other Christians are seeking the support of European institutions – not least the European Parliament – but again with scant success. Yet in the midst of much pessimism, one still finds prophetic Iraqi voices the likes of Fr Meyassir, a Chaldean Catholic priest, who advised his congregation, "Be careful not to hate the ones killing us because they know not what they are doing. God forgive them".

Alarmingly enough, though, it seems that the policies of intimidation and / or division of Middle Eastern Christians are turning them broadly into sitting ducks in some parts of the region. Only this week, a massive suicide bomb attack against the Coptic Al Qiddissain (Two Saints) Church in the middle-class district of Sidi Bechr in Alexandria, Egypt, resulted in deaths and injuries. Moreover, Archbishop Bechara Rai, President of the Episcopal Commission for Mass Media in Lebanon, urged the Lebanese officials to exert their utmost efforts in order to prevent the infiltration of terrorists into Lebanon. Whether wilful or otherwise, and irrespective of the many possible perpetrators and reasons behind those attacks, they are regrettably producing fear in many communities and fomenting tensions between different Christians and Muslims.

One Christmas carol recites the words of the angel, "Glory to God in the highest, and on earth peace, goodwill toward all men". But in many parts of the Middle East, these words will not be conspicuous only by their biblical mistranslation since their warmth and fuzziness will also sound quite hollow. In many hearts and hearths, the woes and hardships of 2011 will be at the forefront of peoples' daily realities. They will worry about their lives and livelihoods and wonder if their children and grandchildren will ever discover the elusive peace and harmony that the carol proclaims during this season.

But such a breakthrough requires men and women of responsibility to nurture enough good will in order to help foster an inclusiveness leading toward peace – be it in Israel–Palestine, Iraq or the region as a whole. Only then will the prospect of the future become more encouraging.

28 December 2010

Chapter 24

The Holy Land Coordination

The Holy Land Coordination (HLC) is a bit of a mouthful and might even sound a tad pretentious. But in the words of its organisers and facilitators, this acronym brings together a bench of Catholic bishops from Europe, North America and South Africa who travel to the Holy Land every January for a few days. It was set up at the end of the twentieth century upon the invitation of the Holy See, and its key purpose is to visit and support Arab Christian indigenous communities in the Holy Land.

A persuasive initiative

In the releases by Alexander DesForges, Head of Media at the Catholic Church, three P-words have come to express the remit of the HLC: Prayer, Pilgrimage and Pressure. Perhaps there should also be a fourth P though: Presence. The bishops are indeed present every year, and by their very presence they hope to remind the 'Living Stones' (1 Peter 2. 4-5) of the Christian communities in the Holy Land that they are not forgotten by their brothers and sisters in the other corners of our global village. After all, do these communities not often remind us in the West that they feel like the 'Forgotten Faithful'?

Pilgrimage is one of the most transformative aspects of this annual journey. The bishops going to Israel, Palestine and Jordan do so to visit those local Catholic communities and share in their Sunday liturgy, meet their civic leaders or local politicians and engage with their parishioners. Over the years, the visiting bishops (I often refer to them as the flying bishops, but not in the Anglican sense of the word!) have often heard pleas for more pilgrims to come from their home countries in order to show solidarity with the local communities. In fact, there has been a concerted effort on the part of the Catholic Bishops' Conference of England and Wales – the organising body for the HLC – to encourage pilgrimages where people take the time to walk and talk rather than simply jump in and out of tourist buses.

Pressure, a softer version of which might be Persuasion, refers to the work to be done once the bishops go back home where they speak to their own governments, deputies or parliamentarians, Israeli and Palestinian ambassadors and – more critically – the media about a wide range of issues blunting the lives of local Christians. In so doing, those members of the HLC delegation underline the need for dignity, justice and peace for those communities in Israel, Palestine, Jordan and across the whole MENA region.

In January 2016, for instance, the organisers of the HLC chose to focus on the vulnerable Christians in Gaza and Beit Jala who often experience marginalisation, disenfranchisement and even ostracism from their own communities. The focus also fell this year on the refugees from Iraq and Syria in Jordan.

From a faith-centred perspective, or at least on paper, all this might sound quite impressive. But what are the real strengths and weaknesses of such a delegation that visits the Holy Land year-in-year-out?

Solidarity and togetherness

I suppose that the three or four P's guiding this movement undergird the very ethos and strength of the group visiting those different towns and meeting with the differing communities. There is a sense of solidarity and togetherness that energises Arab Christians who see their fellow believers from faraway climes telling them their woes are not ignored and that they are part of the Oneness of the Body of Christ. However, there are in my opinion four critical points where the Holy Land Coordination has the opportunity to redouble its efforts.

The meetings in the Holy Land should be more ecumenical and must go beyond the Catholic constituencies in an attempt to interact with other Churches. After all, the Holy Land is a *koinonia* of thirteen traditional churches, and focusing only on the Catholic dimension at the expense of the other communities – be they Greek Orthodox, Syriac and Armenian Orthodox, Lutheran or Anglican – diminishes the outreach and effectiveness of such a potent movement.

The HLC remains quite hierarchical in its approach. The meetings gravitate around the leaders of churches or communities. I would be much more heartened if they meet the plethora of NGO's and CRO's that are doing such a wonderful job in Israel, Palestine or Jordan – in terms of justice and peace issues or else for the refugees that need more attention. In fact, some of the Israeli and Palestinian NGO's have a more astute understanding of the realities in the Holy Land than church leaders whose very vocation could be self-limiting at times.

The visits should also be more proactive and daring in terms of their inter-religious dimension. It is a fact that Christians do not constitute more than a few meagre percentage points of the overall populace in those biblical lands.

Christians, as I have often stressed out in the past and much to the annoyance of some leaders, are devoutly Christian by faith but broadly Muslim by culture. In our troubled world today, with the Arab uprisings, no appreciation of the Christian presence and witness could be complete without introducing the Muslim component into it.

Moral example and persuasion

Finally, and perhaps much more significantly, the Bishops who take part in the HLC travels should be willing to speak out boldly and without equivocation about the injustices they witness during their travels. After all, they are not politicians massaging their words and cherrypicking their ideas. They can opt to speak out the whole truth instead – starkly and unabashedly if necessary – whether about the vagaries and excesses of the Israeli occupation of Palestinian lands or the growing fear of radicalism by Islam and its wearying effect upon those small Arab Christian communities – even if this leads to some arguments with officialdom. Tiptoeing around those issues in order not to offend anyone, or conversely saying too much with an exiguous understanding of the issues, are both counter-productive and do not subscribe to those four ethical P's. As Pope Francis has shown the world since 13 March 2013, it is vital at times to cause discomfort and not be weak-kneed with our responses.

In conclusion, the Holy Land Coordination distinguishes itself as a unique and highly laudable project for bringing the considerable moral weight of the Catholic Church and its social teachings into play. But it should recall the eight Beatitudes that Jesus spoke of in his Sermon on the Mount. So how much of an impact will those annual travels have depends largely on the flying bishops themselves and their organisers.

11 January 2016

Chapter 25

Palestine: what goes around comes around

"As you sow, so shall you reap" and "what goes around comes around" are pretty much the basic understanding of how the personal and political experience of cause and effect operates most times in our lives – particularly as we acknowledge and reflect on it.

So ... after cutting $200 million in Palestinian aid in August 2018, US President Donald Trump decided to cut a further $25 million from hospitals serving Palestinians in Jerusalem. Mind you, the official statement was that it was "redirecting" this aid money (which amounts in EU currency to just under €22 million), but do let us not quibble over semantics.

I suspect that Palestinians were not jolted by this latest cruel gesture from a mercurial president who often views political conflicts as a balance sheet of credits and debits. But no matter the levels of anticipation or surprise, this latest gesture will also impact five hospitals in Jerusalem. Two of those – St John's Ophthalmic Hospital and the Augusta Victoria Hospital – are well known to me personally, from my time as a kid in Jerusalem (Jordan at the time). Besides, both hospitals have assisted needy Palestinians over many decades, and I can still recall the queues of Palestinian patients going into those two hospitals in order to undergo eye surgery or else to receive treatment for cancer.

A punishment operation

So it might sound mean – no, venal – that the US would cause so much human suffering. Or does it? One suggestion is that the US Administration is punishing the Palestinian Authority headed by Mahmoud Abbas in Ramallah for its refusal to discuss the so-called 'deal of the century' that Jared Kushner, Jason Greenblatt and David Friedman are stapling together. After all, just look at the consecutive steps that were taken over the past few months. The US Embassy has been transferred from Tel Aviv to Jerusalem. Financial aid to UNRWA has been chopped off drastically. The Right of Return for refugees is being gradually eroded away from the negotiating table. The PLO Mission in Washington DC has been shut too, and the US Ambassador in Israel never misses an opportunity to repeat that Israel can do whatever it wills with settlements. Much of this runs contrary to International law, human rights laws and accepted norms of diplomacy or legitimacy. Yet, in one year, the Trump Administration have become political gunslingers aiming at Palestinians without any compunction about the impact on ordinary Palestinians. After all, the leadership can insulate itself from hardship and so will not be the ones to wince from the pain of such decisions.

Sadly, attempting to remove those core issues from the negotiating table, and bullying traditional partners or even the ICC in the process, is not the politic way of brining the Palestinians back to the negotiating table. Nor does it define any long-term strategy that strengthens a two-state solution – assuming we are still even talking of two states living in peace and security next to each other. After all, such actions remove whatever hope there is of a peaceful resolution and begs the question as to what Palestinians are meant to negotiate over? Their total and abject surrender?

I have followed this conflict since the early days of the now-defunct Oslo chapter, and I have seen moments of hope and others of despair along the way. However, I have rarely come across such despondency, resignation and weariness as I sense today among ordinary Palestinians. Even the attempt by some Palestinians to break a political taboo by entering into a coalition with Israeli Jewish partners and running in the municipal elections in Jerusalem in October reeks more of exhaustion than of boldness. Yet, these decentralised efforts to deal with their existential challenges are one way for Palestinians to defy brutishness and to find alternative solutions to their endemic problems.

Beyond despair

So what can happen in the future? The Trump Administration is wedded hook, line, and sinker with the Israeli objective of neutering the Palestinians completely so that they end up having a "state minus" at best that is no more than blobs of disjointed lands held together by the largesse of Israel and the wink and nod of some states. Call it autonomy without sovereignty. This wilful and complicit collaboration aims to morph a political conflict into a humanitarian issue. It needs to be resisted by Palestinians with the help of the EU and other states, organisations or movements that are concerned about the repercussions of another unlawful re-jigging of geopolitical realities in the region.

As you sow, so shall you reap: this popular phrase traces its roots to

Galatians in the Christian New Testament. It has stood the test of time for some two millennia. So despite a horizon that is bereft of encouragement, Palestinians can still take heart that – to paraphrase an opinion piece written by Hussein Ibish recently – they might be knocked down once more but they will not glibly be knocked out no matter the constellation of forces against them. To me that spells hope no matter the dankness of the moment – for both peoples.

11 September 2018

Chapter 26

The 2019 Knesset elections: against all odds?

Is he the new king of Israel? Is he perchance a political prestidigitator? These were just some of the chants from Israeli Prime Minister Benyamin (Bibi) Netanyahu's supporters as he relished his electoral victory. After all, had he not managed to win the latest Knesset (parliamentary) elections in his country despite all the odds being stacked against him? That said, it was not an outright victory, as you and I would probably define it, since his Likud party won a mere 36 seats but in so doing he managed nonetheless to outrun the main Blue and White (in Hebrew, Kahol Lavan) coalition by one seat in the 120-seat parliament.

However, the result was also a symbolic victory over a serious challenger party that tried to define itself as being more centrist and that had three retired generals (Benny Gantz, Bogie Yaalon and Gabi Ashkenazi) as its key founders. But far more importantly, he won because if one tots up the numbers, Netanyahu could garner a ten-seat lead over his adversaries in the next parliament in view of the preponderance of right-wing and extreme right-wing parties over the five leftist or Arab ones in the new parliament.

It is quite true that his coalition partners will exact a heavy price from Netanyahu in return for their support of his premiership, but they will nonetheless still join his government in the end. And Netanyahu will have secured his fifth mandate and will be on course to become the longest serving prime minister of Israel by outlasting David Ben-Gurion who served as prime minister for the periods 1948-1953 and later 1955-1963.

Bibi's attempted firewall

It is in fact quite remarkable that a man who faces a pending criminal indictment on bribery and fraud charges by the Attorney-General (likely to come down later in 2019) can still be the victor. But whilst Netanyahu got his wish to be the star of Israeli politics, he will also concede to the demands of his ultranationalist partners not only because of any shared ideological affinities but far more critically because he needs their support to firewall himself against the legal charges that might otherwise take him to Maasiyahu Prison in Ramla like former prime minister Ehud Olmert in 2016.

Netanyahu also had powerful friends and allies backing him, chief among them US President Trump, Russian President Putin and Brazilian president Jair Bolsonaro. In the lead-up to the elections, Trump offered Netanyahu Jerusalem and the Golan Heights (in clear contravention of International law), Putin helped repatriate the remains of an Israeli soldier who had been missing since the war of Lebanon in 1982, and Bolsonaro visited Israel and gushed at the airport in Hebrew *Ani ohev et Yisrael*, or "I love Israel". Moreover, Netanyahu made sure to burnish his right-wing credentials further by 'promising' that he would not dismantle any settlement – big or small – built illegally on Palestinian lands. Rather, he promised almost as a casual aside that he would annex the West Bank, although the geographical space for such an annexation remains unclear.

So a lot of jingoistic fireworks, an array of populist promises, and a result that tows Israeli politics further to the right. In fact, Netanyahu could easily join the ranks of the Orbans, Salvinis and Morawieckis in his drive for fake news were it not for one pesky but hugely irritating problem for him: there are almost three million Palestinians living in the occupied Palestinian territories of East Jerusalem, the West Bank and Gaza. Indeed, Netanyahu is keen to spread his wings, schmooze with the US President and AIPAC, gather many frequent miles by vising the Russian president or embrace, whether overtly or covertly as many Arab rulers (leaders is a bit of an exaggeration for some of them) and prove that Israel is an enduring and kingly miracle – just like him. Were it not again for those stubborn and persistent Palestinians who refuse to lie down, surrender their rights, and accept that he tramples on them.

Re-profiling Palestinian aspirations
In fact, it troubles me that the Palestinian issue has been relegated in the overall political focus of many countries. The USA, for all intents and purposes and at all levels, is no longer an honest broker but an ally of Israel. So much so that the new envoy to combat anti-Semitism, Elan Carr, has even stated that boycotting goods made in Jewish settlements in the West Bank is anti-Semitic even though the settlements themselves are illegal under International law.

The EU on the other hand is so busy with its internal European ructions that it hardly has the space for any concrete initiatives over the Israeli-Palestinian conflict. Besides, it has often seen its role as a banker than a political bellwether. And a number of Arab countries, whether in the MENA or Gulf regions, have distanced themselves from the Palestinians' political aspirations because they are fixated on Iran. The enemy of my enemy being my friend is a proverb originally from the Arthashastra that some Arab countries apply to Israel when it comes to the perceived Iranian threat.

And of course there are the Israelis and the Palestinians themselves. Israelis have become far too inured to the pain of occupation that they no longer worry too much about it. Their wall and the self-righteous proclamations of some of their politicians, when coupled with Palestinian dissensions, seem to endow Israelis with a false sense of security. But what goes round comes round and those millions of Palestinians are not going anywhere – no matter how many of them emigrate or however many Jerusalemite (blue) Identity cards are confiscated on spurious grounds and however many houses are demolished too. The olive trees that some settlers uproot from Palestinian lands are the very same trees that keep Palestinians attached to their national dreams for self-determination.

But Palestinians are suffering the consequences of an insidious occupation, coupled with global apathy and internecine power plays. So in the next few weeks or months, once the coalition-building barter is over and Netanyahu has secured his tenure, Jared Kushner, aided and abetted by his two lawyers Jason D Greenblatt and David M Friedman, will unfurl the US 'deal of the century' and hail it as the ultimate deal.

The 'deal of the century' is a trap
This document fills me with a sense of dread. Although a closely-guarded secret, this purportedly 60-page document will not – cannot – meet Palestinian hopes no matter how glibly it is marketed by its geneticists. I have not seen all of the document myself, but I would nonetheless posit that it will not refer to East Jerusalem as the capital of a new Palestine or to the right of return for Palestinian refugees. Rather, it might (and I use the conditional clause on purpose) entail the annexation of Area C of the West Bank (around 60% of the arable lands) and the substitution of the land-for-peace strategy that has been the cornerstone for peace since 1967 with one that prioritises economic incentives. The thinking would presume that throwing money at a problem – in this case the Gaza Strip that is home to well over a

million Palestinians – will make Gaza residents more emollient to the idea mooted for it to become the new showcase for "Palestine". And the West Bank would revert to its Judaea and Samaria status whilst housing separate and desperate pockets if Palestinians.

An exaggerated scenario? Perhaps. But everything I have read or discussed fails to inspire me with confidence that the so-called deal could be an even-handed breakthrough. Rather, I smell the coffee and it is rancid. Israel might well be asked to make some compromises although the likes of National Union leader Bezalel Smotrich have already stated that they will bring down Netanyahu's government rather than accept any peace plan that establishes a 'terrorist state' next to Israel. However, any Israeli compromises would pale into insignificance when compared with what Palestinians might be expected to forfeit in terms of their core and sovereign demands. And forfeit they cannot because Jerusalem is also ingrained in the psyche of ordinary Palestinian Muslims and Christians. The poem "In Jerusalem" by the late Mahmoud Darwish echoes the resilient attachment of Palestinians – "forgetting to die" he writes – to their lands.

The pendulum will swing again

So where to now? Unless Arab countries and their representative organisations wake up from their self-induced slumber and rework their priorities, and unless Europe acts more robustly to salvage Palestinian hopes for freedom, we are inevitably heading for more tensions – and eventually for an eruption that would not be pretty. The feeling of invincibility that Israel feels today could become brittle or illusory, and the sheer impunity of its actions invites consequences no matter the brashness of the moment. Does the ancient Book of Samuel not hold some clues?

Is Netanyahu the political genius that will lead Israel to its abyss – as an *Haaretz Weekly* podcast (Episode 22) mooted recently? As the world watches Beit Aghion in the Rehavia neighbourhood of Jerusalem and contemplates the Prime Minister's political sleights-of-hand both as king and magician, Palestinians and their friends will instead see in him a chancer who is trashing their legitimate hopes for dignity in their own homes and for sovereignty on their own lands.

But why should Israel care, you might well ask? Well, it should care because the stark alternatives are either the inevitable emergence of a binational state with equal rights under the law for Israelis and Palestinians which is anathema to Netanyahu and his political acolytes. Or it would lead to a relentless colonisation of Palestinians that, no matter how repressive and relentless, will eventually find its South Africa moment.

Irrespective of Israeli intransigence, or of Arab and international inaction, I would lay odds that the pendulum will swing again. And I will conclude with a thought by Archbishop Emeritus Desmond Tutu of South Africa who said on the Today programme at NBC television on 9 January 1985, "I am not interested in picking up crumbs of compassion thrown from the table of someone who considers himself my master. I want the full menu of rights." Prophetic?

15 April 2019

Afterword: Hope Revisited

The articles in this book tackle the Israeli-Palestinian conflict from a variety of angles over a range of topics across a period of two decades and more. If they have a common explanatory strand, it is about trying to clear away some of the confusions which mask the real, core issues that need addressing. The muddling of our thought and perspective comes in a number of ways. This concluding chapter seeks to address some of these confusions, and in so doing to point us ever more firmly in the direction of a realisable hope for the future of both Israel and Palestine – more pointedly, of Israelis and Palestinians.

Religion and politics

In parts of the western world it is often said that politics and religion are the two subjects you should not raise in polite company. They are seen as inherently divisive and therefore socially avoidable. However, as will have become evident throughout this book, without a maturing discourse about power and beliefs in both civil society and the realms of governance, little can be discussed which offers realism or hope about the future of Israel–Palestine. That said, it is important not to confuse or elide these two spheres without careful consideration.

For example, when the Israeli government appropriates huge swathes of land that are Palestinian lands; when it uproots trees that are Palestinian trees for Palestinian farmers – is this a religious act? Are these sources of life being denied because of religion, or are they to do with land and power? This goes to the core of the Israeli-Palestinian context. Fundamentally, the struggle is not about religion. It is not so much an issue between Judaism, Islam and Christianity as it is about who controls the land. All kinds of rationales, secular and religious, may be imported into conversations to support or justify certain actions around this, but these should not take our attention away from the central concern.

What Israel is doing in its current policy trajectory, what it has done in the past, and what it tried to do during the Oslo years and afterwards (one of the reasons that process failed) is, in the words of Afif Safieh – who used to be the Palestinian Head of Mission in London – seeking to retain Palestinian demography while getting rid of the Palestinian geography. That defines the conflict. For most people, it has little to do with American evangelical ideological conceptions that this land is a battleground for dangerous end-of-the world visions that are premised on a battle of faiths.

So while we undoubtedly have to pay careful attention to the use and abuse of religious language and doctrines in the midst of this power struggle, we should not mistake them as the main point of contention. What is at stake is the future of two wounded peoples, as Archbishop Elias Chacour (a human rights advocate who is both a Palestinian and an Israeli citizen) has put it. That is the level at which the-land-and-power conflict must be addressed on human and political grounds.

Power and racism

Another way of clouding the political issue of Israel–Palestine arises from intense debates around anti-Semitism and other forms of racism. A number of clear things need to be said about this. First, the repulsive prejudice of anti-Semitism on the one hand, and legitimate criticisms of (or opposition to) the philosophy and practice and Zionism on the other – these are two different things. It may be that some use the latter as a cover for the former, but that does not mean that opposing anti-Semitism means automatically accepting Zionism, or that rejecting Zionism is automatically endorsing anti-Semitism. We need to be able to separate disagreements about the politics of statehood from the common need to oppose racism in all its forms.

Second, therefore, it is important to point out that the Semitic peoples are both Arab and Jew. For Arabs to be anti-Semites means for them to be against themselves, as well as their neighbours. It simply does not make sense. Viewed this way, we are dealing with a family divided. The way to restore relations between Jews and Palestinians is to recognise their common as well as individual humanity, to face up to the divisions of colonial history, to accept the constraints of International law, and to propagate a politics which rejects oppressive violence and does justice instead.

Speaking personally, I would want to defend to my dying day (to adapt the famous phrase of Voltaire) the right of every single Jew to have his or her own dignity, independence, politics and personhood. But what I would also defend is my right, and that of others, to criticise Israeli official politics and policies. Again, one does not necessarily lead to the other. If we want to look responsibly at anti-Semitism, we do not look at the roots of anti-Semitism in the Levant, but in Europe. We remind people that the Holocaust was not perpetrated by Arabs but by Europeans. We condemn and oppose racism whenever and wherever it is manifested, of course. But we do so in a way that distinguishes racist politics from legitimate aspirations for nationhood and security for all peoples, not just for some at the expense of others.

Israel and apartheid

That in turn, raises the question as to how and in what form a state such as Israel has taken shape, what its nature is at this point in history, and what prospects it offers both Jews and Palestinians. Is Israel, as some would now contend, an inherently and institutionally racist state based on the subjugation of one people by another on an ethnic basis? This question has come into focus recently with the introduction of the Basic Law: Israel as the Nation-State of the Jewish People, informally known as the Nation-State Bill or the Nationality Bill. This is an Israeli Basic Law that specifies the nature of the State of Israel as belonging to the Jewish people. The Knesset adopted this Law with 62 in favour, 55 against, and two abstentions, on 19 July 2018. It has been met with sharp criticism internationally, including from several prominent Jewish-American organisations, on account of defining the state on overtly ethnic grounds, thus reducing non-Jewish citizens to second-class citizens.

Regarding the use of the term apartheid (Afrikaans for separate development) and comparisons between Israel and South Africa during its institutionally racist era, I personally do not like the use of sweeping terms. Big words bring out the resistance of some people to talk, to dialogue, to negotiate. If I come and tell you that you are a fool, but I would like to talk with you, you are going to take offence and resist examining behaviour which may indeed turn out to be foolish, but which does not forever have to define our relationship or your actions. When I talk to you and seek to show you that what you are doing is not right, and is indeed actively harmful, from my perspective, there is at least an opportunity to move forward and make change.

So is what is happening in Israel apartheid? You can see reasons for saying so (as distinguished figures such as ex-US President Jimmy Carter and Archbishop Emeritus Desmond Tutu have done) and reasons for balking at using that term (as others have said). But what I would want to say without getting into a pointless polemical argument about terminology and political analogy is that, materially and demonstrably, there is an insidious occupation going on of one people by another. This has gone on for over fifty years. Eventually, in occupations of this nature, when one people is humiliated and subjugated in order to raise up the other people, then the victim and the victimiser alike end up paying the price. As far as the Basic Law is concerned, it is clearly a racist Law. Some have argued that it is 'purely symbolic'. But it is hard if not impossible to deny that it has effect, and that the effect is prejudicial and damaging. It gives predominance of Jews over Arabs, and Israelis over Palestinians, in terms of language and rights. That is unacceptable.

If you look at the relation to occupation of the land and the ugly Separation Wall let alone other measures such as the confiscations of Jerusalem (blue) IDs for Palestinians or the random closure of the hundreds of *machsoms* (roadblocks) that can be found everywhere into the West Bank and amongst its towns and villages, you see clearly what is happening. If you talk to people in Bethlehem, where Christian tradition and Scripture has it that Jesus Christ was born, then you begin to hear and see the reality, as the artist Banksy did when he made his impression on the Wall and put his imagery on the 'Walled Off Hotel' near the separation wall. You can understand from all this how Palestinians are made to feel. So if I were pushed hard to use the word apartheid I could do so, but instead I would prefer to say that Israel adopts racist policies towards the Palestinians, and if people do not want the word apartheid used, then what needs to happen is that the policies must change.

Addressing fears

So what of the Israeli fear that some people wish to abolish not just the state of Israel but the Jewish people in the region and beyond? Is there any truth in that?

Again, it is better to be guided by the reality on the ground, rather than to use big words which act as a block on change and the development of renewed relationships. First, I would want to say that I can well understand the fears and insecurity of a people who saw six million of their people exterminated during the Second World War. That trauma continues to live in many people. As an Armenian dealing with the legacy of our own Holocaust during the First World War, I completely understand this. It is horrific. Many Armenians, especially of the older generations, far more than the younger generations, still hanker about something that was lost. Younger Armenians, in contrast, are often happy to be part of the diaspora, and to retain their identity while becoming fully citizens of the country in which they now live. So in a sense Armenians are looking towards what happened to them in Anatolia, just as Palestinians are looking at the destroyed lemon tree and the loss of the keys to their property when the land was stolen away from them during the Israeli advance that led to the creation of the state of Israel in 1948. So now many Israelis also live with insecurity in their heads. But we need to look at the source of such insecurities and how they can be addressed justly. This cannot happen without historical understanding and attention, once more, to material realities.

Right now it would be ludicrous to suggest that there is a prospect of the abolition of the state of Israel. If anything, the opposite is true. Israel has nuclear weapons which none of their other neighbours have, as well as massive military might let alone an ironclad American support. So the idea that Israel can be obliterated simply does not stack up, and anyone who uses this to thwart reform, change and acknowledgement of the grievances and rights of Palestinians is doing so for covert political purposes – ones which, in fact, make Jews in the region less rather than more secure, ironically. This is part of the complex web of tragedy and injustice that defines the Israel–Palestine conflict.

Regarding the hostile words from Iran, and the nuclear question there: it is important to realise that the Iranians are not Arabs, and in fact there are Arabs fighting Iran as much as Israel is. It is a matter of huge regret that the Iran nuclear deal has collapsed, under the weight of a sharp change of tack from US President Donald Trump, whose policy shift in the region makes matters much worse. But a lot of the Iranian rhetorical response to this, and its language against Israel, is mere bluster. So the best answer to verbal threats from Iran or elsewhere is to build a just and sustainable peace in Israel–Palestine, to take away the source of grievances and to seek the healing of all peoples in the region on this basis.

Two states or one?

The practical realisation of hope resides in renewed relationships and political solutions. The two have to go together. How that can be so has been the underlying concern of many of my articles in this volume. But to what end in relation to Israel–Palestine? One state or two? This is a crunch question. For many years there has been a feeling that a sovereign, contiguous and secure Palestinian state alongside an equally secure Israel is the answer. However, the recent policies of the Israeli government have been militating against this, while still eliding calls for a single secular democratic state for Israelis and Palestinians alike as with 'the abolition of Israel'. This leaves no effective room for manoeuvre, it would seem. Others who believe strongly in a 'two-state solution' are now beginning to doubt whether it can now be viable – politically, economically or (importantly) demographically.

My years of hands-on engagement with the Israeli-Palestinian problem have been on the basis of a two-state outcome. However, the rapacious Israeli policies of colonisation (not least building houses exclusively for Israeli Jews on occupied Palestinian territories) are undoubtedly making thins worse. Recent elected governments in Israel seem to see making Palestinians less secure as an essential part of making Israelis secure – when in fact the opposite is the case. Security for one requires security for all. So we are reaching a situation where, with the best of goodwill, it becomes more and more difficult to look at a map, with its water tables and resources, and work out how you could draw up boundaries for two viable states. The damaging policies of the Trump administration, which are encouraging illegal settlements subsidised and militarised by the Israeli state, is pushing us to a situation where the two-state approach will become impossible. I must stress that we are not there yet, but that is, tragically, the seemingly unstoppable direction of travel.

This is why the whole Palestinian narrative held by the younger generations now is moving away from the one held by the older generations and into a one-state or bi-national solution with equality under the law. Now if Israel is pulling away from a two-state solution, you can only imagine the level of distress and anger that a one-state, bi-national proposal would make. Nevertheless, it is conceivable. However, if sensible Israeli and Palestinian leaders are to come together to work out a compromise on this basis their communities have to put them in a position to do so by marginalising the hardliners (the opposite of what has been happening), and we need to understand that a solution can only work if it guarantees equal rights for Israelis and Palestinians alike, and a place of security for Jews, Muslims and Christians living together. What it cannot do is try to replicate a two-state solution under the guise of a bi-national one.

So, as they say, 'the jury is out' on which way forward can gain traction. My own commitment still remains to the two-state idea at present, but whatever is put on the negotiating table will require a change of heart and mind, especially from the Israeli government. The 2019 re-election of Netanyahu for a fifth mandate on an even fiercer rhetoric does not make that likely in the immediate future, but as we have seen in the realm of global politics, all kinds of unexpected things can happen, and in the meantime it is important to go on seeking to influence the opinions and possibilities we can control, rather than lamenting or being immobilised by those we cannot.

Religious persecution and exceptionalism

At the beginning of this chapter I warned against certain kinds of confusion between religion and politics, and the false notion that the core of the Israeli-Palestinian conflict is religion, when it is clearly land and power. Nevertheless, the role and status of religious communities, not least minority ones such as the various Christian communities, is a not unimportant factor in the future of the region. As someone who has been a spokesperson and advocate for the different churches as part of my own journey, their fate is naturally (and personally) a concern of mine. In recent times a discourse around 'persecution of Christians', in particular, has grown up. Is this a helpful way of framing the issues, it may be asked?

This is a matter for the whole Middle East. Israel–Palestine has its won set of variables. But if we look at the larger picture, over the nine years of the Arab Spring (which has now turned into an Arab autumn because of the way it has been hijacked) Palestinians have been talking both about their own rights and also those of Christians and others in Iraq and Syria, for example – particularly Syria. Of course we should struggle for the rights of Christian communities across the whole MENA region, as we should for all other communities, religious or otherwise. But a sense of exceptionalism, Christian or otherwise, is profoundly unhelpful. In this context, some church leaders have hidden under the protection of rulers who behave in despotic ways towards others in order to preserve, they believe, their own communities. This is an approach which is damaging to the prospects of being part of a more just society, alongside others.

Exceptionalism is to be objected to from an ethical and spiritual perspective (in the gospels Jesus challenges such behaviour), but also from a pragmatic point of view. A time of change could well come when Muslims turn round to Christians and point out that while they were being killed, imprisoned and tortured for resisting oppression during the Arab Spring, church leaders were cosying up to the regimes doing that very killing, imprisoning and torturing. The danger here is that history will repeat itself and Christians will find themselves staring at more violence against themselves. Whereas, from the depths of Christian history, we should understand the meaning of *martyria* (which means both martyrdom and witness), and find ourselves able to stand honestly in solidarity with all who are persecuted or oppressed.

The Arab Spring, human rights and migration

While it is undoubtedly the case that a key to unlocking the wider dilemmas of the MENA region is a settlement in Israel–Palestine, development elsewhere in the Middle East also rebound on that conundrum. So the course of the Arab Spring has been significant for the past few years. Some now pessimistically call this an Arab winter, but as I have already said, I feel the term autumn is more appropriate. Things could still go in a number of directions. The West is implicated in both the fate of the Arab nations and that of Israel and Palestine, naturally. On the positive side, I believe that there is still a strong sense of the importance of human rights in the West. That has been a feature of policymaking, but it has often been compromised or supplanted by short-term commercial and economic interests, and by a valuing in political terms of stability over freedom and at times of interests over principles.

It is noticeable that there was some enthusiasm in Europe for the Arab uprisings at first, but that was soon tempered by fears of chaos, the rise of Islamist groups taking advantage of what has effectively become a multi-agency civil war in Syria and elsewhere, and the perceived risk of new regimes of a more threatening nature to Western interests arising across the region. So repression in places such as Egypt and Saudi Arabia has been glossed over and even aided and abetted through continued arms sales and the like.

Equally, Europe itself is not stable at the moment, and forced migration from areas of conflict and human rights abuse has become a controversial political issue, with Chancellor Angela Merkel's principled stand for human dignity and refuge being undermined from within, and the EU moving to adopt a harsh approach to its borders with the rest of the world. So given what was seen as a choice between freedom and stability, many Western nations seem to have chosen stability.

All this is widely seen as another betrayal by peoples across the Middle East and North Africa. There is also a political and historical inability in the West to understand not only that 'the migration problem' is infinitely more challenging in MENA countries, but also that it is a consequence of the longer term damage caused by colonial policies and attitudes in the past. So we need to look at all those millions of

Palestinian refugees still spread across Lebanon, Palestine, Jordan let alone Turkey and even some now in Iraq, Syria and Egypt. If that, for many years, remains unresolved it scares the West as much as it scares the region itself.

The place of Arab Christians

Arab Christians are an important part of the MENA region. They come from there and actually predate Islam, for example. In that sense, no one can doubt or question their authenticity or identity. The fact that they have a political vision which is similar, to a large extent, to what ordinary Muslims feel across the area was made manifest in Palestine when US Vice-President Mike Pence visited Israel in 2018.

Pence wanted to go to Bethlehem to identify with Christians there. But they refused to meet him and they declined to open the door of the Basilica of the Nativity – a very clear exemplification of what they thought of United States policies toward Israel and Palestine. So those two things go hand-in-hand: Christians are part and parcel of the region, but they are not *the* region. An 'us' or 'not us' attitude is therefore not appropriate, either for Christians or those with other religious backgrounds.

A dangerous shift in political imagination

What is happening post Trump and the rise of populism across Europe is a phobia about migration stirred by the far right which leads to the idea that 'if we do not support these troublesome people, they will not come'. That is a wholesale misunderstanding. Even worse, what has gradually developed over the last few years is this insularity occurring at the very moment when – for the first time in years – the Arab political space has been preoccupied with something other than Israel–Palestine. If you had looked at NGOs and churches operating in the region in the past, for example, and asked 'where do the programmes and money go?', the answer would be to assist Palestinian refugees. When the Arab Spring erupted there were other concerns – Libya, Syria, Egypt, Tunisia and their quest for democracy. There was a multiplicity of conflicts and possibilities which not only made the West look at the region a little differently, but which also meant that the citizens of those counties (who were – and in their majority still are – fully and vocally supportive of justice for the Palestinians) became so much immersed in their own pains and agonies that they had less time to give to the Palestinian cause. So gradually, during the Arab Spring, the centrality of the Israel–Palestine conflict as the hub within the Arab political imaginary in the region diminished.

Add to that the fact that Trump came and convinced some Arab rulers in the Gulf, in Egypt and elsewhere, that the real enemy is not Israel but Iran. Therefore, what is happening now is that the Middle East is being framed as a place not where there is a struggle between Israelis and Palestinians, but where there is a conflict between Arabs and Iranians. This is very worrying because not only does it change the narratives and dynamic of the region in terms of geopolitics, but also it makes it far more volatile in terns of what could go wrong.

So a month ago, for example, there was a meeting in Amman, Jordan, of all the heads or speakers of parliaments across the Arab world. The aim was to support the Palestinian people and to emphasise the centrality of Jerusalem for all Muslims and Christians as well as Jews. But some started to argue that the real issue was not this but Iran, even though Iran was not on the agenda. This feeds a certain US paranoia, and the whole bloated, over-exaggerated Trump agenda starts to take over.

This has led to, and been part of, developments such as the closing of the Palestinian mission in Washington DC, defunding UNRWA, ending funding for medical services, stopping support for dialogue projects and more. All this is to try and bully the Palestinians and their allies to accept what America wants to dictate to them. That is, in turn, what Israel is telling the US is *its* agenda. At the moment this means Netanyahu's expansionist policies. What people are not taking on board in the midst of all this is that while some rulers – in places like Saudi Arabia and the United Arab Emirates – have bought into this narrative and are very happy to work with Trump (and perhaps even Netanyahu) on isolating Iran further, the peoples of the region still hold the Palestinian issue as being quintessential to the MENA as a whole. That is where there is a tug of war between rulers who are trying to change the narrative (for what they perceive as their own political and economic interests in the court of the US) and ordinary people who are saying 'no'. So further incendiary gaps are emerging between governors and governed.

Israel–Palestine as the key

Notwithstanding these further levels of conflict and smoke-screening, we need to remain clear that a resolution to the Israeli-Palestinian conflict is, and remains, central to addressing all the other conflicts across the MENA region. There can be no escaping this. So long as injustice against the Palestinians prevails and persists, so long as one people in Israeli occupies and rules over another to prevent them having their right to self-determination, this is going to be an open sore. This is so not only for people in the region, but for Muslims across the wider world. Therefore, if the sore is not healed, but instead is denied, worsened or merely treated with a Band-Aid, nothing fundamental will change. In fact, the situation is likely to get worse for all concerned. The difference between Israel–Palestine and the Arab Spring is that in the former it is one people subjugating another people, whereas in the latter it is rulers subjugating their own people.

Confidence building on the road to hope

So where do we go from here, and what is the source, shape and project of hope from my perspective? Let us begin with some practicalities. What we have seen lately has been a collapse of sensible, confidence-building and trust-restoring measures within the region. These badly need to be reinstated. As we have observed above, you cannot have confidence or grow trust when one people constantly accede to policies that subjugate another. In a sense, then, while it is necessary to adapt one's thinking to changing and tumultuous circumstances, my own underlying thought about what needs doing has not changed over the past two decades.

That is, if we are to retain the genuine hope of an independent Palestinian state next to Israel, with contiguity, security and all that follows (as much for Israelis as for Palestinians, please note), then the roadmap to that end needs modifying rather than abandoning. That is what is involved in moving from a Palestinian state on paper at the United Nations, to one in reality. For example, we need to take account of, and address, the problem of illegal settlements. This is profoundly difficult, but it is not an obstacle that can be ignored. It is more than a tweak, but less than a revolution. It is not conceivable to ask people to gather up their belongings and head back to borders from before 1967. That is not going to happen.

Now it would be ideal if we could go back to the Palestine that existed during the British mandate, where Jews and Arabs lived together in the same land. But the Balfour declaration and the British authorities messed that up, and the consequences have been negative ever since. However, politics is the art of the possible not the ideal. At present it is about negotiating a way between the ideal (a bi-national state where the rights of everybody are equal under the law) and various flawed versions of a two-state resolution. Maybe in the future the ideal will become more possible, but at the moment we do not have the luxury of dealing with fond imaginings but with difficult realities that must be shifted so that people can find a space to live in with a modicum of justice. Hope can take this life-giving, pragmatic shape, too. It is not always about grand dreams.

Moreover, a two-state solution is not impossible, as some say. Regarding the settlements, before Trump the way they had been built and expanded meant that if you looked at the map carefully (and Palestinian cartographers have done that carefully), it was still possible to have two states living side-by-side. What I am worried about is that this is changing now, because Netanyahu feels emboldened to go further, backed by Trump. It is imperative that international pressure is applied against this. Moreover, it is not up to Israel to decide what is good for Palestinians. They should have their state based on a parcel of land that is their own, and if they then want to contend among themselves that becomes an intra-Palestinian issue not an Israeli-Palestinian one. In the meantime, what must be contended is the core idea that Netanyahu is furthering (through the Basic Law), that of several tiers of citizenship in Israel – so that you have the Jews first, then the Arab Israelis, then the Jerusalemite Palestinians, then the West Bankers, then those in Gaza. This is no solution, but a continuation of subjugation.

There are entrenched problems here, undoubtedly. But what history shows is that either a people has to be wiped out (genocide) or you have to do a deal. I am sorry to put this so starkly, but we must face reality. That too is part of practical hope. I am not a maximalist or an "impossibilist" (if I can throw in a neologism here), but someone looking for a base from which to move forward reasonably and positively. That was the attempt of the Oslo process. The important point here is that in a compromise it has to be win-win. If it is win-lose it will not be sustainable, and if it is lose-lose there is no point in even starting the conversation.

In the end it is very simple. If you want to give security to the Jewish people, give security to the Palestinians. That is win-win. But waking up to it can be hard, and is as much a human aspiration – and I would say a spiritual and moral one – as it is a political task. The majority in Israel can be persuaded to accommodate, I believe, but at present they are being confused and led by a hard-right agenda from their leaders, while the peace movement and the peace agenda are weak. Investing in an alternative that reaches out and persuades people to think again is another feature of the practical hope we need.

Those who are presently frightened about the possible consequences of giving Palestinians rights are being corralled by Netanyahu, but there is a core of the electorate who would go for a win-win solution if it was presented to them. The problem is that they are not being offered it. What they are offered are walls which might protect them today, but which cannot do so forever. It is bridges that we need – including those towards the right, because it is they who may finally be seen as reliable enough to carry forward a peace plan (rather than the left, who are seen as weak on security) by a majority. There are perhaps some lessons here with the Northern Ireland peace process, where it was the harder line unionists in the shape of Ian Paisley who had for years said 'no' and were finally persuaded to say 'yes'. That meant that the left had to think differently and on a larger canvass, too. But it proved a breakthrough, albeit a fragile one.

Hope in and through *anamnesis*

But now we need to go much deeper. For while hope is indeed to be found in negotiation, moral pressure, envisioning alternatives and working pragmatic solutions, a larger change is undoubtedly needed – that of the human heart and of human communities. Let me put this personally. Hope springs eternal, it is said, almost casually – but how, exactly? As a Christian I have to answer by saying that it happens as the crucifixion leads to the resurrection. It happens because the mystery of a God deeply engaged with human suffering and wrongdoing is also the mystery of a God who gives life where no life is expected or even possible. I cannot say how others discern and fathom this hope, only that I feel its truth and carry it on the path I travel. It is the core of Christianity, without which it would collapse, as would my own convictions.

Alongside this I believe in the inalienable rights of all people for self-determination. If a people like the Palestinians, who have been suffering under the yoke of oppression and subjugation all these years can still long for freedom and fresh air (not mere recycled air), then there is hope. That is the human way of expressing it. And as Archbishop Elias Chacour has said, the human hope and the divine hope meet at the point in which Israelis and Palestinians may be able to see each other not as enemies, but as two wounded peoples who have the capacity and need to recognise each other in that woundedness and seek healing together. That is what a Christian would mean by 'kneeling at the foot of the cross of Christ', for example.

Another important biblical word here is *metanoia,* conversion, turning around and heading in a new direction which offers life rather than death. This is realised wherever people invest in hope – in conversations between persons across the divide, in articles and broadcasts, in the work of humanitarian and religious agencies and NGOs, in myriad small ways that create new possibilities and fresh understanding. What we have to do is to prepare ourselves for a new reality that can come when it is least expected. (There is much in the Christian story about this, too.) That requires persistence and perseverance, which are disciplines and, as various wise ancestors have said, virtues. There is hard work to be done to keep faith with hope, and to make it live in the face of despair. That is as far as can be imagined from a facile optimism that simply wishes things to get better or believes, on the basis of no examination and little investment, that a breakthrough will somehow come tomorrow anyway.

Equally, you need a catalyst for change, and that means some person or persons who can encourage Israeli and Palestinian leaders (and the West) to want a different future, such that they are prepared to start with something rather smaller along the road. I think of an Israeli mother and a Palestinian father, both of whom lost sons at the hands of the other community. They came together and travelled to London and elsewhere to say, "We *can* forgive and we *can* move forward, in spite of it all". Such voices can have deep impact on those hardened by politics, but only if the incentives are there – people-to-people contact, yes, but also plans that can gain political traction. There is a reciprocal necessity here. But the leverage for forward movement is lacking at the moment, because on the larger scale the US is not acting as a fair arbiter and the Europeans have stepped back too much – being willing to provide humanitarian assistance, but not offering the kind of political vision that can break open a deadlock in a spirit of partnership. Here is an invitation and a challenge to *metanoia.*

In conclusion, one of my few inspirers has been Michel Sabbah, who was the Archbishop and Latin Patriarch of Jerusalem from 1987 to 2008, the first non-Italian to hold this position in more than five centuries. He was also a friend, and he used to say two things. First, the Holy Land is a land not for exclusive possession, but for two peoples and three religions. I say that now too. Second, he used to say that the Christians of the region are a people of the cross, and that it is their duty to carry the cross – to bear suffering hopefully – until the day of resurrection. This too is my conviction. In Orthodox theology it is a Eucharist *anamnesis* (a re-membering, a bodily appropriation of the deep mystery of hope) which brings together the Passion, Resurrection and Ascension of Christ. That is the source of my hope, for living out in the daily struggle for life in the face of death, and for being lifted up when we have been cast down.

This chapter has been created through conversation and cooperation between the author and the editor.

About the Author

Dr Harry Hagopian is an international lawyer, ecumenist and political consultant. He also acts as Legal Consultant to OTS Solicitors in London (particularly on Brexit and immigration issues). He is an Ekklesia associate and regular contributor (http://www.ekklesia.co.uk/HarryHagopian). Formerly Executive Secretary of the Jerusalem Inter-Church Committee and Executive Director of the Middle East Council of Churches, he is now an international fellow, Sorbonne III University, Paris, and author of *The Armenian Church in the Holy Land* (The Russell Press). Dr Hagopian's own website is www.epektasis.net – follow him on Twitter here: @harryhagopian and on Facebook here: https://m.facebook.com/MENA.analysis/

Other contributors

Editor and interviewer: **Simon Barrow** is Director of Ekklesia. He is an author, commentator, journalist and educator. From 2000 to 2005 he was Executive Secretary of the Churches Commission and Assistant General Secretary of Churches Together in Britain and Ireland, in which capacity he worked with Dr Hagopian.

Foreword: **Rami G. Khouri** is Journalist-in-Residence and adjunct professor of journalism at the American University of Beirut (AUB), where he is a Senior Public Policy Fellow. He is coordinator for AUB in the NYC Briefings Initiative, a Syndicated columnist for Agence Global Syndicate, USA, and Nonresident Senior Fellow at Harvard Kennedy School.

Select Bibliography

The following books, articles and resources are referred to throughout the text:

Alternative Information Centre, 'Israeli occupation forces and settlers continue to commit human rights violations against Palestinians in the West Bank district of Hebron' – June 2018 report, one of a monthly series (AIC, 2018). http://aicnews.org

Ben-Meir, Alon, 'Israel's Continued Independence Rests on Palestinian Independence', *Huffington Post,* 1 July 2012.

Borger, Julian, and Beaumont, Peter, 'Defiant Donald Trump confirms US will recognise Jerusalem as capital of Israel', *The Guardian,* 7 May 2017.

Cohen, Hillel, *The Present Absentee: The Palestinian Internal Refugees in Israel since 1948* (Institute for Palestine Studies, 2003). Translated from Hebrew into Arabic. Hebrew edition, 2000, o.o.p.

Ehrenreich, Ben, *The Way to the Spring: Life and death in Palestine* (Penguin, Harmondsworth, UK, 2016).

Fisk, Robert, 'Edward Said: an icon and an iconoclast', *The Independent,* 27 September 2003.

Haaretz Podcasts, 'Netanyahu – the Political Genius Leading Israel Into the Abyss' (*Haaretz Weekly,* 10 April 2019).

Ibish, Hussein, 'How Palestinians Should React When Trump Unveils His Peace Plan' (*Forward,* 2 May 2019).

Read more: https://forward.com/opinion/423659/how-palestinians-should-react-when-trump-unveils-his-peace-plan/

Karmi, Ghada, *In Search of Fatima: A Palestinian Story* (Verso, London, UK, 2002).

Hagopian, Harry, *The Armenian Church in the Holy Land* (The Russell Press, London, UK, 2017).

Halper, Jeff, 'The narrow gate to peace', *Sojourners,* August 2005.

International Crisis Group, *The Emperor Has No Clothes: Palestinians and the End of the Peace Process,* 7 May 2012, https://www.crisisgroup.org/middle-east-north-africa/eastern-mediterranean/israelpalestine/emperor-has-no-clothes-palestinians-and-end-peace-process

Kairos Palestine Document: A Moment of Truth (Kairos Palestine, 2009).

Kassab, Elizabeth, *Contemporary Arab Thought: Cultural Critique in Comparative Perspective* (Columbia University Press, 2010).

Laird, Elizabeth, *A Little Peace of Ground* (Macmillan, 2003; reprinted by Haymarket Books, London, UK, 2006).

Moules, Noel, *Fingerprints of Fire, Footprints of Peace: A Spiritual Manifesto from a Jesus Perspective* (Circle Books, 2012).

Raheb, Mitri, *Faith in the Face of Empire: The Bible Through Palestinian Eyes* (Orbis, Maryknoll, NY, USA, 2014).

UN Fact-Finding Mission on the Gaza Conflict, *Human Rights in Palestine and Other Occupied Arab Territories: Report of the United Nations Fact Finding Mission on the Gaza Conflict* (United Nations, 2009) – https://digitallibrary.un.org/record/666096

About Ekklesia

Ekklesia is an independent network providing 'thought space' for exploring the impact of ethics and beliefs in the areas of public and social policy.

We want to encourage transformative local engagement with global issues – not least among moral communities (churches and other groups) who see themselves as being firmly committed to people at the margins.

Our operational values are those of social justice, inclusion, nonviolence, environmental action, participative democracy and creative exchange among those of different convictions (religious or otherwise).

Ekklesia is active in promoting – alongside others – new models of mutual economy, conflict transformation, peacemaking, social power, restorative justice, citizen action and truth-telling in public life. This means moving beyond 'top-down', colonial approaches to politics, economics and beliefs.

While strongly influenced by the Peace Churches and grassroots movements for social change, Ekklesia is keen to work with people of many backgrounds who share common principles and approaches.

Ekklesia's reports, news analysis and commentary can be accessed via our website (www.ekklesia.co.uk) on Twitter (Ekklesia_co_uk) and on Facebook (www.facebook.com/ekklesiathinktank/).